The
Peace Chiefs
of the
Cheyennes

The
Peace Chiefs
of the
Cheyennes

BY STAN HOIG

Foreword by Boyce D. Timmons

UNIVERSITY OF OKLAHOMA PRESS
NORMAN

BY STAN HOIG

The Sand Creek Massacre (Norman, 1961)
The Humor of the American Cowboy (Lincoln, 1970)
The Western Odyssey of John Simpson Smith (Glendale, 1974)
The Battle of the Washita (Lincoln, 1979)
The Peace Chiefs of the Cheyennes (Norman, 1980)

Library of Congress Cataloging in Publication Data

Hoig, Stan.
    The peace chiefs of the Cheyennes.

    Bibliography: p. 179
    Includes index.
    1. Cheyenne Indians—Biography. 2. Cheyenne
Indians—History. I. Title.
E99.C53H63   970'.004'97   79-4739

Contents

Illustrations

ILLUSTRATIONS

Foreword

"Let us keep our land in peace and grant us the right to our own religion, language, customs, and culture. We do not wish to be a whiteman." These words were spoken to me by Cheyenne Chief Ralph Goodman in 1967, a few years before his death. He was repeating the pleas made by his forefathers years ago, and today a majority of Native Americans desire the same goals. This land was invaded by Europeans who were seeking these rights and privileges. How sad that today the nation is still striving for goals that were the pleas of the American Indian over two hundred years ago.

Few white men have ever been able to understand the American Indian, and few have made any attempt to do so. I have been very privileged and honored to have participated in certain phases of Cheyenne culture and religion. I have experienced some of the sensations and emotions that are expressed by the Cheyenne chiefs in this book. They had and still have an unshakable faith in their philosophy of life and in their ultimate destiny. The non-Indian is finally realizing that, because of their cultural heritage, American Indians have a special relationship to all things, a oneness or unity of body and spirit that has made it possible for them to endure unbelievable hardships and oppression.

The Cheyenne concept of the "circle of life" encompasses the significant aspects of other cultures and religions and provides an inner peace the Cheyenne cannot find in other societies. Early pioneers, frontiersmen, missionaries, government agents, and soldiers misinterpreted almost every Indian custom. They had never participated in the "circle of life," and so they could only report what they saw based on their own cultural experience.

This book does not attempt any interpretation of the lives or beliefs of the Cheyenne chiefs. It provides the background that resulted in Cheyenne action or speech, and the reader is free to draw his own conclusions.

Before you read the book, ask yourself why the American Indian has retained a strong and dominate culture in the face of the tremendous effort of a superior force to destroy it. Ask why the American Indian and his way of life have received such high respect and admiration throughout this country and the world.

Great wisdom, intellect, and love are expressed by these remarkable Cheyenne chiefs, and if you enter their tipi with an open heart and mind, you might have some understanding of the great "circle of life."

BOYCE D. TIMMONS
Adopted Cheyenne Chief

Preface

There has always been the notion, very much mistaken, that
Indians are humorless, emotionless beings. Their stoicism has
become proverbial. The Cheyenne chiefs who were seen at
councils and other meetings with the whites bore themselves
with such stately grace and solemn dignity that they often appeared beyond such human behavior as laughter or weeping.
But, in truth, the Cheyenne chief, like other Indians, was altogether as human as anyone else, displaying an excellent sense
of humor and perhaps more compassion than most.

In 1879, for instance, six captured Cheyennes were taken to
Kansas to face trial on the charge of killing Kansas settlers during the famous northward trek of Little Wolf and Dull Knife
from Darlington Agency. While being held at Lawrence, Wild
Hog, Old Man, Blacksmith, Left Hand, Run Fast, and Meheha
were taken to visit a touring circus from London, England. There
the chiefs saw a variety of wild animals from around the world,
including elephants, lions, camels, Bengal tigers, and other
forms of animal life they had never seen before. The Indians
studied them without expression. When the American lion, red
deer, and brown bear were displayed, however, the Cheyennes
pointed westward to indicate that they had seen those animals
before in the Rocky Mountains. The prisoners were delighted
with the horseback riding, astonished that white men could ride
so well. But it was the clowns, one lean and one fat, that caused
the Cheyennes to shake with laughter. Blacksmith laughed until
he cried, dispelling the notion that Indians did not laugh or cry
the same as all other men.

The Cheyenne chief loved his family, his children, his people.
He simply disciplined himself to control his passions in line with
his responsibilities as a leader. Thus the image he presented—
and it was by no means a false image—was that of a man of
self-control, of quiet, reflective wisdom, of dedication to the
good of all rather than to base and selfish motives. In so doing,
the Cheyenne chief provided an ideal of leadership that was

Northern Cheyenne chiefs at Dodge City, Kansas, in April, 1879, following their escape from Fort Robinson. *Top row:* Tangle Hair, Left
Hand, Old Crow, and Porcupine. *Bottom row:* Wild Hog, interpreter
George Reynolds, Noisy Walker, and Blacksmith. The chiefs are
typically stoic here. When they were taken to see a circus later, Blacksmith cried with laughter at the clowns. *Courtesy of Kansas State Historical
Society, Topeka.*

more noble, perhaps, than that of "civilized" man. But the problems faced by the Cheyenne leaders of the nineteenth century were overwhelming.

Perhaps the most singular story of the American West was the struggle of the Indian leaders to prevent the extinction of their tribes as they became caught in the irrepressible crush of white civilization. The Cheyennes, a small but warlike and prideful tribe ranging over the central plains, faced the main force of white migration westward. They gave welcome to the first white explorers and traders, but as the numbers of the intruders increased, so did the difficulties. The chiefs witnessed the debauchery of their people by the white whisky traders, the gradual restriction of their land area, the killing off of the wild game by which the Indians subsisted.

Then came the massacre of their band at Sand Creek and the realization that the whites had declared war against them. They were driven from their hunting and camping grounds in Colorado, then from the prairies of western Kansas, and finally to a refuge in Indian Territory. Their warriors struck back in anger, committing savage but ineffective war against the whites of the frontier. The white men were too many, their armies too strong. The Cheyennes, without food or ammunition, were driven to the reservation and forced to submit to the white people's government. Eventually the reservation system was disbanded, and the Cheyennes were given the right of citizenship.

Today they remain an impoverished people, unable and unwilling to move fully into the mainstream of American society, knowing that if they do they may well disappear as a people. Stubbornly they hold on to their Cheyenne identity, enduring the present, remembering the past.

This book is indebted to all those who through history have met, known, and reported on the Cheyennes; to historians of the Cheyennes, such as Grinnell, Berthrong, Llewellyn, Hoebel, Dorsey, Powell, and others; to adopted Cheyenne Chief Boyce Timmons for his counsel; and to the archivists, librarians, and curators who rendered great service in making research materials available. In this case I would like to acknowledge, especially, the generous help of Mr. Joe Snell of the Kansas Historical Society; Mr. Jack Haley of the University of Oklahoma Division of Manuscripts; Mrs. Alice Timmons, formerly of the Phillips Collection of the University of Oklahoma Division of Manuscripts; Mrs. Alene Simpson, Mrs. Manon B. Atkins, and Mrs. Martha Blaine of the Oklahoma Historical Society; Ms. Elaine Everly of the National Archives; and Mrs. Dorthea Ray of the Oklahoma's Central State University Library.

Special appreciation must also be acknowledged to my wife, Pat Corbell Hoig, whose help in critical evaluation, typing, footnoting, and copyreading has, as always, been invaluable.

STANLEY W. HOIG

Edmond, Oklahoma

The
Peace Chiefs
of the
Cheyennes

1

Chiefs of the Cheyennes

The Peace Keepers

Though your son might be killed in front of your tepee,
you should take a peace pipe and smoke. Then you
would be called an honest chief. You chiefs own the
land and the people.

The Legend of Sweet Medicine

The warm southerly winds and longer days had melted the last patches of winter's snow into the land and sucked up green shoots of grass and wild flowers to color the prairie. The earth stirred with the appearance of game and bird life, and the tribal hunters returned daily with fresh meat for the camp kettles. It was time for the renewal of the chiefs of the Cheyenne Nation. Runners were sent out to the scattered bands of the tribe carrying the red invitation sticks that indicated that a council was to be held.

At the appointed time and to the appointed place, they came. The young men rode in first, dashing their ponies about, whooping and singing and firing their guns. Then came the family groups—the older men, the women, the children—their horses dragging the two-pole travois laden with lodge covers and camp gear. From cradleboards on the backs of blanketed Cheyenne women peered the round, wondering faces of Indian babes. In the rear, marked by billowing clouds of dust, trailed the enormous herds of ponies and mules that would virtually cover the surrounding hillsides when grazing.

Soon all the bands had converged and taken up their assigned positions in the tribal circle; hundreds of lodges, their exteriors decorated with drawings and their crisscross pole tops silhouetted against the sky, surrounded a hugh central clearing. Before each tipi stood tripods of long willow sticks supporting buffalo-skin war shields, scalp-draped lances, and, dangling in the center, bead-and-quill-worked parfleche medicine bags. A great chiefs' lodge was erected in the middle of the clearing, its door facing

3

Historical Trace of the
Cheyenne Nation

MONTANA

Fort Union

Little Missouri

Knife

Heart

Cannonball

NORTH DAKOTA

②

④

③

⑤

Black
Hills

Cheyenne or Teton

Fort Pierre

SOUTH DAKOTA

Bighorn

Tongue

Powder

㉗

㉕

Crazy Woman Fork

㉘

Missouri River

Shyenne River

Minnesota River

Mississippi River

MINNESOTA

①

Pine Ridge Agency

NEBRASKA

Fort Robinson

Fort Laramie

⑨

㉚

Fort Robinson

WYOMING

North Platte

Fort McPherson

Platte River

Council Bluffs
Omaha

IOWA

Fort Sedgwick

South Platte

⑭

㉑

⑱

㉙

Fort Kearny

Platte Trail

Republican

Fort Riley

St. Joseph
Fort Leavenworth

Westport

Port St. Vrain

Denver

⑫

⑬

⑩

Smoky Hill

Solomon

Saline

Fort Hays

⑪

Fort Harker

MISSOURI

Sand Creek

Bent's Fort

⑧

Fort Wallace

⑯

Walnut Creek

Fort Zarah

Fort Larned

Santa Fe Trail

⑮

Fort Lyon

Arkansas River

Pawnee Fork

Fort Dodge

⑰

KANSAS

COLORADO

Cimarron Cutoff

Camp Supply

Cimarron

INDIAN
TERRITORY

㉔

ARKANSAS

Taos

⑦

North Canadian

㉖

Darlington Agency
Fort Reno

㉒

NEW MEXICO

Wolf Creek

㉓

⑳

⑲

South Canadian

Washita

Fort Cobb

Fort Sill

㉕

North Fork

Red River

TEXAS

MAJOR EVENTS AND LOCATIONS OF CHEYENNE HISTORY

Number on map	Event	Date
1	Cheyennes, first known in Minnesota area, visit Sieur de La Salle's fort on Illinois River.	February, 1680
2	Cheyennes arrive in North Dakota area.	ca. 1700
	Two separate village sites have been identified, one village massacred by northern tribes.	ca. 1730 and 1784
	Jean Baptiste Trudeau visits North Dakota Cheyennes.	1795
3	Cheyennes move to Black Hills region.	Early 1800's
4	Alexander Henry and Charles Mackenzie visit Cheyenne village.	1806
5	High-Backed-Wolf and others sign friendship treaty with United States at mouth of Teton River.	Spring, 1825
6	Tribe splits and Southern Cheyennes arrive on Arkansas River.	Before 1830
7	Battle of Wolf Creek (Cheyennes and Arapahoes defeat Comanches and Kiowas.)	1838
8	Cheyennes and Arapahoes make peace with Comanches and Kiowas at Bent's Fort and win right to range south of Arkansas River.	1840
9	Treaty of Fort Laramie, second Cheyenne treaty with United States	1851
10	Colonel Edwin V. Sumner attacks Cheyennes on Solomon River.	July, 1857
11	Lieutenant George S. Eayre murders Lean Bear, touching off Cheyenne hostilities.	Summer, 1864
12	Black Kettle, White Antelope, and Bull Bear visit Denver for peace council with Governor John Evans.	September, 1864
13	Sand Creek Massacre (Colonel John M. Chivington attacks Black Kettle's village); Yellow Wolf and White Antelope killed.	November, 1864
14	Cheyennes attack wagon train at Fort Sedgwick.	February, 1965
15	Treaty of Little Arkansas	October, 1865
16	Major General Winfield Scott Hancock burns deserted Cheyenne-Sioux village on Pawnee Fork.	April, 1867
17	Treaty of Medicine Lodge	October, 1867
18	Battle of Beecher's Island; Roman Nose killed.	September, 1868
19	Battle of the Washita; Black Kettle killed.	November, 1868
20	George Armstrong Custer rescues two white women on Sweetwater River; Slim Face captured and later killed.	April, 1869
21	Tall Bull's village destroyed and the chief killed by troops under Major E. A. Carr.	July, 1869
22	Darlington Agency established.	May, 1870
23	Battle of Adobe Walls	June, 1874
24	Hennessey wagon train burned by Cheyennes.	July, 1874
25	Colonel Ranald S. Mackenzie's campaign against the Cheyennes.	Fall, 1874
26	Sand Hill fight	June, 1875
27	Battle of Little Bighorn	June, 1876
28	Mackenzie attacks Dull Knife's village on Crazy Woman Creek.	November, 1876
29	Dull Knife and Little Wolf retreat north.	September, 1878
30	Dull Knife's people break out of Fort Robinson.	January, 1879

the rising sun like all the others. Now the camp crier, trailed by naked boys and barking camp dogs, rode about the vast encirclement calling out in his stentorian voice the news of a meeting of the Council of the Forty-four.[1]

When the sun was mid-high in the morning sky, the chiefs began moving toward the great lodge. They were proud, stately men with bright feathers perked above their heads. Their long, black braids, carefully wrapped and decorated with silver disks, hung over their shoulders and down the front of their blankets or fringed buckskins. Some wore breastplates made of porcupine quills, and a few displayed the silver peace medals given to them by the Great Father when they had visited him in Washington. Large copper earrings hung from slits in their ears, and most wore armlets as well as rings.

These men walked tall, with great dignity of bearing, as became their positions as chiefs of the Cheyennes. Their bronze, wide-structured faces were strong with the resolve that comes to men who know no fear. Most had been great warriors as younger men. Most had ridden into battle many times and counted coups against enemy tribes. But now for each the ways of war were past, willed to the younger men of the war societies, who must win their own laurels of victory. These men were the peace chiefs of the Cheyennes. As members of the Council of the Forty-four they had the task, individually and collectively, of helping maintain peace within and without the tribe.

Inside the lodge the Principal Chief seated himself crosslegged upon the robes spread there, facing the lodge entrance. The others took their places at his side in the order of their position in the encampment, forming a large circle. When they had all seated themselves, the tribal priest brought forth his bag of kinnikinnick and opened it onto a cloth on the ground. He mixed the kinnikinnick well with herbs, bark, dried leaves, and the marrow of buffalo bones. When the red-clay ceremonial pipe with its long stem, lavishly decorated with beads and quills and feathers, was filled and lighted, the priest conducted a long, solemn harangue to the sky spirit (Heammawihio, or the Wise One Above), to the earth spirit (Ahtunowhiho, or the One Who Lives Below the Ground), and to the wind spirits who dwelled at the four points of the compass. The movement of the pipe was in a crisscross fashion.[2] When he had finished, the priest handed the pipe to

6

the chief at the head of the circle, who took several long draws upon it, blowing puffs of smoke upward each time toward the Wise One Above. Then the pipe was patiently passed from chief to chief slowly around the circle, each chief making his signs with the stem, until the pipe had been returned to the starting point.

Now it was time for talk. A tribal elder rose to his feet and announced that the day had come for him to step down as a chief. He named the one he had chosen to take his place. After a moment of silence another chief took the floor and gave his views. No one interrupted his speech, which was made with a combination of the Cheyenne tongue and the graceful hand motions of sign language. An occasional grunt of approval came from the circle of somber faces that surrounded the speaker. When this chief had finished, another rose and the chiefs continued in turn until all who wished to speak had spoken. Finally the matter was decided; the new chief was accepted. He would be expected to give his predecessor a gift and later, during the feasting and celebrating, to prove his generosity even further by making presents of horses and robes to poor people in the tribe. But first the new chief must be told the story of Sweet Medicine, the mythical tribal hero who according to legend appointed the first chiefs of the Cheyennes. "Listen to me carefully," Sweet Medicine advised,

> and truthfully follow up my instructions. You chiefs are peace-makers. Though your son might be killed in front of your tepee, you should take a peace pipe and smoke. Then you would be called an honest chief. You chiefs own the land and the people. If your men, your soldier societies, should be scared and retreat, you are not to step back but take a stand to protect your land and your people. Get out and talk to the people. If strangers come, you are the ones to give presents to them and invitations. When you meet someone, or he comes to your tepee asking for anything, give it to him. Never refuse. Go outside your tepee and sing your chief's song, so all the people will know you have done something good.[3]

Though the circumstances of tribal legend vary, the primary virtues prescribed here for a Cheyenne chief are valid. A Cheyenne chief was required to be a man of peace, to be brave, and to be of generous heart. Of these qualities the first was

7

unconditionally the most important, for upon it rested the moral restraint required for the warlike Cheyenne Nation.

Few whites on the western frontier ever understood that the Cheyenne chief was essentially a man of peace. Generally he was understood to be primarily a ruling monarch who maintained autocratic control over his people and, secondarily, the war leader of the Cheyenne fighting men. Not many whites have recognized that the chief's authority was primarily a moral authority, subject to the respect accorded him by the people, that it was the war societies who controlled the fighting men and led them into battle, or that keeping the peace within and without the tribe was the chief's principal responsibility.

Under ordinary conditions a chief's influence might be effective, but during times of crisis when relations with the whites were bad, there was often little the chief could do. As early as 1851 reporters at the Treaty of Fort Laramie wrote that the Dog Soldiers were evidencing a haughty disregard for the authority of their chiefs and for the military power of the whites. "They form a war party," wrote one observer, "and often go to war upon their own hook, sometimes without the knowledge or consent of the chiefs. They are so numerous, and so well banded together, that the chiefs can do nothing with them."[4]

Following the killing of Chief Black Kettle at the Washita River in 1868, General Philip H. Sheridan and Lieutenant Colonel George Armstrong Custer sought to justify the act by blaming Black Kettle for depredations committed on the Saline and Solomon rivers of Kansas by a war party, some of whose members were from Black Kettle's camp. Black Kettle had admitted afterwards to Brevet Major General William M. Hazen that he had not been successful in keeping his young men at home. The Saline-Solomon raids may have been justification for Sheridan's winter campaign, but there is no evidence that Black Kettle was responsible for the raids or deserving of the charges made against him after his death. On the contrary, there is repeated evidence of Black Kettle's many attempts to preserve peace between the Cheyennes and the whites who invaded Cheyenne lands.

The peacemaker role of the Cheyenne chief can be detected throughout the recorded history of the tribe. In the following chapters it will be evident time and again that the Cheyenne

8

chiefs were dedicated to reconciliation between the Cheyennes and the whites. They knew that the Cheyenne Nation had to bend to the overwhelming force of white civilization or perish. Tragically, the peace chiefs were often caught between the warring elements of their own tribe and those of the whites.

It is a truth of western history that many of the leading Cheyenne chiefs were killed by whites as a result of their role as peacemakers, not simply because they were for peace but because whites erroneously held them responsible for the acts of the war societies. Because they were peaceful, the chiefs were more easily found and attacked than were the warring elements of the tribe. Old Tobacco was shot and killed by a teamster while attempting to warn a wagon train of a Comanche war party. Lean Bear was shot down without warning by United States troops while conducting a peaceful buffalo hunt. White Antelope, Yellow Wolf, Standing-in-Water, One Eye, and War Bonnet were massacred while supposedly under the protection of United States troops at Sand Creek. Little Rock was killed by Custer at the Washita along with Black Kettle. All these chiefs were proven peace advocates among the Cheyennes.

The virtue of bravery was unquestioned for a chief of the Cheyennes. Most of them came from the six military societies, and from boyhood they had been trained to be daring and fearless warriors. Their physical courage had been tested many times in intertribal wars with the Comanches, Kiowas, Pawnees, Utes, Crows, and others. They were men such as Custer described when he ordered the Cheyenne chiefs seized in his camp on the Sweetwater River in 1869. During the flurry of excitement following Custer's order, one tall, broad-chested Cheyenne calmly stood by, taking arrows from his quiver, thumbing their steel points to test their sharpness, and eyeing the shafts for trueness.[5] There was little fear in a Cheyenne warrior.

No better example of chieftain courage could be found than in the act of One Eye when he brought to Fort Lyon a letter from Black Kettle in 1864. When told by the fort commandant, Major Edward W. Wynkoop, that he had been fortunate not to have been shot approaching the fort, One Eye answered:

> I knew it. . . . I am young no longer. I have been a warrior. I have not been afraid to die when I was young; why should I be when I

am old. Therefore the Great Spirit whispered to me and said: "You must try and save your people," and I said to the Council of our head chiefs, "Give me true news, such as is written to carry to the chiefs of the Fort," and I am here.... I thought I would be killed, but I knew that paper would be found upon my dead body, that you would see it, and it might give peace to my people once more.[6]

In 1867, Black Kettle attended the Medicine Lodge peace councils despite threats made against him by the Dog Soldiers. Following the massacre of whites along the Saline and Solomon rivers of Kansas by a drunken party of young Cheyennes, Arapahoes, and Sioux in 1868, Chief Little Rock willingly gave Wynkoop, then the Indian agent, full details of the affair. He also agreed to turn over the guilty leaders of the party, though he knew that to do so would be very dangerous for himself and his family.

That the Cheyenne chiefs possessed the virtue of generosity is also supported by an abundance of historical evidence. Lewis Garrard, who visited the Cheyennes during the winter of 1846–47, told how he and trader John Simpson Smith were given the hospitality of Chief Slim Face's lodge during their stay and were even provided with the choice position at the back of the lodge, where one escaped the annoyance of others passing in and out. The white man was always welcome with the Cheyennes, Garrard claimed, and he would be provided with water or hot coffee and food.[7] Even in more difficult times, whites met with such generosity. In 1868, Dog Soldier Chief Bull Bear, though he knew scouts William Comstock and Abner S. Grover to be spies on his village northwest of Fort Hays, Kansas, followed Cheyenne custom, fed the two men, and gave them the protection and shelter of his lodge.[8]

Black Kettle is known to have used his own horses to purchase white captives from other bands in the cause of peace. When he met with the peace commissioners at the mouth of the Little Arkansas following the Sand Creek Massacre, he told them that whenever he met white men on the plains, "I give them my horse and my moccasins, and I am glad today to think that the Great Father has sent good men to take pity on us."[9]

Grinnell describes this characteristic of generosity in a

Cheyenne chief as a part of his dedication to the best interest of his people:

> A good chief gave his whole heart and his whole mind to the work of helping his people, and strove for their welfare with an earnestness rarely equalled by the rulers of other men. Such thought for his fellows was not without its influence on the man himself; after a time the spirit of good-will which animated him became reflected in his countenance, so that as he grew old such a chief often came to have a most benevolent and kindly expression.[10]

Grinnell's general observation inescapably finds illustration in Wynkoop's description of Chief Black Kettle during their meeting on the Smoky Hill River in 1864:

> I looked around upon a circle of dusky faces, and saw them all, with one exception, an angry scowl. Their dark eyes were flashing. . . . there was one exception to these ferocious looking faces; it was the countenance of one, whom I knew to be the most powerful among the Nomadic tribes, one whom I could now see since my prejudice had fled, had been created a ruler; one who had stamped upon every lineament, the fact that he was born to command, he while all the balance of the council were like snarling wolves, sat calm, dignified, immovable with a slight smile on his face. He saw my bewilderment, I might say trepidation, and as his eye caught mine, he gave me a look of encouragement which assured me more than if I had the knowledge of a thousand bayonettes within call.[11]

The Council of the Forty-four was the ruling body of the Cheyenne Nation. It was comprised of four chiefs from each of the ten bands of the tribe plus four who were the principal chiefs. Though many of those chosen were members of war societies, a Cheyenne could not retain such membership after being named a chief. The selection of the chiefs was not made by a vote of the people, but rather the Council of the Forty-four was a self-perpetuating body that named its own successors. Usually a chief chose the one to take his place, but the position was not necessarily hereditary in nature. Chiefs sometimes appointed their own sons but were often reluctant to do so.

The chiefs were named for periods of ten years, and councils were held every four years for the purpose of choosing replacements for those who had died or become too old. Though a principal chief could speak for the tribe, action on important matters depended upon a vote of the entire council. The chiefs of the various bands had the primary responsibility for decisions about moving camp and choosing new locations. But such matters as alliances and treaties required lengthy discussions by all the forty-four.

In 1861, when the six chiefs signed the amended version of the Treaty of Fort Wise, which was scorned by the Dog Soldiers, Black Kettle and the others gained the nickname of the "Six Chiefs" among the tribe.[12] But at Medicine Lodge in 1867, when the influence of the Dog Soldiers dominated, Bull Bear remarked, "One is enough to sign for our nation."[13]

The power of the chiefs depended upon circumstances. Following the murder of Chief Lean Bear in 1864, the Dog Soldiers overrode the desire of Black Kettle and other peace chiefs and made war. When Wynkoop met with Black Kettle on the Smoky Hill River some months later, however, the Cheyenne principal chief had the personal persuasion to overcome the antagonism of the Dog Soldiers, who were angry that Wynkoop had brought troops with him. It is interesting that One Eye, determined that his word as a Cheyenne not be broken, even threatened to join with Wynkoop if the Dog Soldiers started trouble.

The system of the Council of the Forty-four was supported by the Cheyennes' religious belief in the Medicine Arrows. There were four sacred arrows, two for hunting and two for war. The Indians believed that an act against tribal taboo, such as murder, would defile the power of the Medicine Arrows and that only banishment of the guilty one for at least four years would uphold their strength. No warrior wished to diminish his war medicine. Thus a control over quarreling and fighting within the tribe, especially needed for the young warriors, was maintained by tribal custom rather than by the authority of the chiefs.

The power of the Medicine Arrows could also work to limit the power of the chiefs. Chief Porcupine Bear, for example, became involved in a drunken fight and killed a man. He was banished from the tribe as an outlaw, and even though he was present at the Treaty of Fort Laramie in 1851, he did not sign the treaty document.[14] When High-Backed Wolf ran from his lodge in 1834 to take part in a family quarrel and was stabbed to death, the people said that he was to blame because as a chief he should have stayed out of the matter.[15] Much later, when Little Wolf killed a man in a drunken argument over the other's attention to Wolf's daughter, the old chief voluntarily exiled himself from his people and lived out of his life away from the tribe.[16]

The Reverend Rodolphe Petter, a Mennonite minister who lived among the Southern Cheyennes around the turn of the century and studied them and their language extensively at Colony Mission, provided some information on the chieftain system. Petter saw a competition for power between the chiefs and the tribal priests:

> In the former days, when the Southern and Northern Cheyenne were one body, they had forty four chiefs, elected from time to time. It happened that some of the older chiefs were reelected, while not a few of the ex-chiefs took further part in the councils as advisors to the new body. The rule, however, was that forty new and four of the older chiefs be selected, the latter as head chiefs of the tribe. Altho priests and chiefs were not the same men, the first had often a greater influence than the chiefs themselves. Especially the Arrow Keeper and his men swayed a greater authority than the chiefs. The present Arrow keeper is a shining example of the usurpation of headman's authority by his priestly influence. The council of the forty four chiefs chosen from the different warrior bands was symbolized by a bundle of forty four red painted invitation sticks, kept with the ceremonial arrows.[17]

Custer's description of his meeting with Chief Medicine Arrow on the Sweetwater River in 1869 supports Petter's view of priestly influence:

> Medicine Arrow hurried me to his lodge, which was located in the center of the village, the latter being the most extensive I had ever seen. As soon as I had entered the lodge I was invited to a seat on one of the many buffalo robes spread on the ground about the inner circumference of the lodge. By Medicine Arrow's direction the village crier, in a loud tone, began calling the chiefs together in council. No delay occurred in their assembling. One by one they appeared and entered the lodge in order of their ranks. I was assigned the post of honor, being seated on the right of the Medicine Arrow, while on my immediate right sat the medicine man of the tribe, an official scarely second in influence to the head chief.[18]

Garrard, in 1846, had also witnessed a display of rank shuffling inside a Cheyenne lodge:

13

We sat in our places at the back part, and the Indians, according to rank, took seats to our left, on mother earth or their own robes. To the right was our host; and, if a man entitled to notice by right of seniority or daring deeds of valor entered, those inferior in honors gave place next to thé white man (us). Sometimes Indians of equal rank were in the lodge at the same time, and then a *sotto voce* dispute as to the "upper seat" would be carried on with much gesticulatory motion.[19]

During the early years of western exploration, before contamination of Indian life by the white man's diseases and whisky, the Cheyennes were recognized as having one of the highest Indian cultures on the plains. White explorers considered the Cheyennes mode of living to be cleaner, their women more chaste, and their sense of personal dignity stronger than most other tribes. Another distinction, not unrelated to the others perhaps, was the chieftain system—a system that demanded Christlike virtues from the men who led the tribe and that produced strong, patient men of calm wisdom and good heart.

2

Host to the Medicine People

High-Backed Wolf

*My father, I believe it was my great father, the
President, who sent you here to talk to us to-day, and
we are glad to see you; we saw troops once before on the
Missouri, and took them by the hand.*

Little Moon

The Cheyennes, a small tribe of Indians who in earlier years had
broken off from the larger body of Algonquian-speaking tribes
abounding north of the Great Lakes and in the eastern United
States, were first encountered by French explorers in the Minnesota region in 1667. Eventually the tribe was driven westward
to the Cheyenne River region of North Dakota by the pressure
of larger tribes from the north who already possessed British
guns. Here the Cheyennes established villages and came to depend upon buffalo for their livelihood. But harassment by more
powerful tribes again forced them southward across the Missouri
River to the Black Hills of South Dakota.

About this time, in the latter 1700's, the Cheyennes became
acquainted with the horse, which then ranged in wild herds on
the prairies. The tall, lithe warriors of the Cheyennes quickly
adapted the animal to effective use in both hunting and warfare,
their new mobility offsetting the force of numbers of the larger
tribes. The Cheyenne warriors soon came to be among the most
feared on the American plains, and before long Cheyenne war
parties were ranging westward to the Rocky Mountains and
southward to the Arkansas River of Colorado, chasing the wild
herds and conducting horse-stealing raids on the horse-rich
southern tribes.

Not much is known about the tribal leadership during the
pre-1800 period, though there were occasional encounters with
the Cheyennes by whites who left some record for history.

Jacques D'Église, Jean Baptiste Trudeau, John Evans, and other traders representing Spain along the Missouri River before 1800 came in contact with the Cheyennes and wrote of the meetings. Trudeau told of an especially interesting encounter in the year 1795.[1] Arriving at the Cheyenne village on the Missouri River that year, he called the headmen together to give them the words of their Spanish Father. He also delivered to them a medal, a flag, a letter patent, and other presents, asking that they choose one member of their band they considered most worthy to wear the medal. The one they chose would be made the great chief of their nation.

The chiefs conferred on the matter and eventually picked a young chief named the Lance. The Lance accepted the medal from Trudeau and promised to do all the good things asked of him by "his Father, the Chief of the White men." Later, however, Trudeau received word that the Lance had done anything but follow the word of the White Father. He had shown a wicked heart, not only for strangers but for his own people as well. He had become angry with other people and treated them badly on every occasion. He had committed murder in his village, killing a Sioux, his wife, and three children who were living among the Cheyennes. The Lance had even eaten and smoked with the Sioux man he murdered. All this, despite his promise to Trudeau to live in peace with the Sioux. Further, instead of keeping the peace with the Mandans and Gros Ventres, the Lance had sent others to steal their horses.

Because of these crimes, the Cheyennes told Trudeau, the great spirits of the medal, the flag, and the letter had become angry with the Lance. Three of his children had died, and lightning had struck the lodge of his own brother, burning it to ashes together with the brother, his wife, children, dogs, and the horses that were tied in front of the lodge. The significance of this tragedy, befalling a chief who had broken his promise to the White Father, had a great effect upon all the other chiefs of the Cheyenne Nation, confirming their belief in the power of the white man's spirits. They denounced the Lance and reproached him for his wicked heart.

Possibly it was this event that led to the practice among some tribes along the Missouri, as mentioned by D'Église, of throwing into the river specially dressed and feathered robes as a sacrifice

to the Spanish White Father.[2] Further evidence indicates that
the attitude of the Cheyennes toward the whites was affected by
the experience of the Lance for a number of years.

The first official contact between the Cheyennes and the
United States government took place in the fall of 1804, when a
part of forty Americans arrived at the Upper Mandan villages
from downriver in two pirogues and a keelboat of twenty oars.
This was the Lewis and Clark Expedition on its way to the Pacific
coast. The explorers came ashore and began building a winter
fort for themselves. On December 2 they were visited by four
Indian chiefs who said they were "Chiens." The white men
smoked with the chiefs, gave them tobacco and an American flag
upon it, and then made a speech advising the chiefs to remain at
peace with the other tribes. In the spring the white men moved
on upstream and were not seen again until the fall a year and a
half later.

The Lewis and Clark party came ashore again on August 21,
1806, near a group of sun-bleached Cheyenne tipis standing on a
hilltop near the mud and grass huts of an Arikara village. Because it was a very warm day, a Cheyenne chief, one of the four
who had met the white men before, invited the leader of the
group into his lodge. After smoking for some time, Captain
William Clark offered the Cheyenne chief the gift of a small
medal. The chief, perhaps remembering the experience of the
Lance, took great alarm at this. He immediately sent for a robe
and some buffalo meat, which he gave to Captain Clark, asking
him to take back the medal. When asked his reason for refusing
the white man's gift, the chief explained that he knew all white
people to be "medicine" and that he was afraid of the medal and
of anything else the white people gave the Indians.

But Captain Clark insisted upon giving the medal to the chief,
saying that the Great Father in Washington had directed him to
deliver the "medicine" to all chiefs who listened to his word and
followed his counsels as proof that he believed them to be sincere and good chiefs. The chief appeared to feel much better
about the matter and accepted the medal. He said that he wished
some white traders would be sent among his people, for the
Cheyennes lived in a country rich with beaver, but they did not
know how to catch them and could not sell them once they were
caught. Captain Clark then promised that the Cheyennes would

soon be supplied with goods and taught the best way to catch the beavers without ruining the pelts.[3]

The Lewis and Clark Expedition was possibly the first meeting between the Cheyennes and the white man that was detailed in writing. The promises that Clark made the chief may well have been sincere, but like so many of the white man's promises they were not to be fulfilled. Ironically, the attitude of the Cheyenne chief (who unfortunately was not named) in fearing the whites to be "medicine" was prophetic. During the century that followed, there would prove to be a fateful truth in this "pagan superstition" of the Cheyennes.

Concurrent with the Lewis and Clark Expedition was a trading expedition by two Canadian traders who were on the Missouri River at the same time as the American explorers. The diaries of Charles Mackenzie and Alexander Henry of the North West Company provide our earliest descriptions of Cheyenne society and culture.

Mackenzie, who had first visited the Mandan and Gros Ventre villages at the great bend of the Missouri in 1804, had met the Lewis and Clark party. But it was on his fourth expedition to the villages in 1806 that he saw his first Cheyenne Indians. A band of "Shawyens or Chawyens" had come to offer terms of peace to the Mandans and Gros Ventres. They were received in friendship by the Missouri River Indians, and as a token of amity the Gros Ventres offered to give up a young Cheyenne who had been taken prisoner in war some years before if the Cheyenne's father would come for him.

The father of the Cheyenne captive arrived at the villages later, accompanied by a number of young men. They brought with them an invitation from the "Great Chief" of the Cheyennes for Rattlesnake, a young chief of the Gros Ventres whom the Cheyenne chief had noticed in battle. Mackenzie noted that, though the Cheyennes had seen and traded with several whites, no traders then resided in their land, and he decided to accompany Rattlesnake and his party to the Cheyenne village.

With a party of some forty Gros Ventres and Mandans and another trader named Jesseaume, Mackenzie crossed the Clearwater, the Heart, and the Cannonball rivers. On the sixth day the party was within a few miles of the Cheyenne camp, and two of the Cheyennes in escort were dispatched to inform the village. Mackenzie's description of the ensuing meeting with the Cheyennes and their chief provides a view of the Plains Indian culture before the advent of the white man's ways:

> We began our slow pace with Rattle Snake and Mr. Gissom, each with his pipe in one hand and the branch of chokeberry, with the fat meat on, in the other, walking before us and singing a lamentable song. The branch and meat were an emblem of peace and plenty, and the pipe, of course, social union.
>
> Many were the ceremonies which we were obliged to observe; at length, we saw several horsemen coming full speed before us and who, on coming to the pipe bearers, stopped short. Rattle Snake, followed by Mr. Gissom, with a humble step and down cast eyes went up to them and held them the pipe from which each Shawyen seemed to draw three whiffs, and then clapped their hands on their breasts as if saying, "It did my heart good."
>
> In this manner they served every one we met with til the Chief arrived with about two hundred horsemen in his suite. The Chief was mounted on a milk-white horse and dressed in his war dress and haranguing the Shawyens as he was coming along.
>
> His followers passed on our right hand and came up behind us, when the chief called out to us to make a general halt. He came down from his horse and embraced Rattle Snake, then, stripping himself as naked as he was the day he came to the world, he clothed Rattle Snake with his flashy war dress and, with the assistance of others, mounted him on his white horse. This done, the chief, quite naked, led the horse by the tether to the camp, six miles off, carrying the pipe in his right hand and the stem pointed towards the camp, singing or lamenting all the way in a language none of us could understand, if there were anything in it to be understood.[4]

Undoubtedly because there was no one to interpret the Cheyenne language, Mackenzie did not identify the chief by name. After a successful trade with the Cheyennes, the North West Company trader returned to the Mandan and Gros Ventre villages. There he was joined unexpectedly by another North West trader, Alexander Henry. Together they accompanied a much larger trading caravan under the Gros Ventre chief Le Borgne, which marched to meet the Cheyenne village now relocated on the Knife River. Henry's journal of the affair tells of meeting some one hundred Cheyenne, Sioux, and Arapaho Indians before reaching the camp.[5] The horses of the "Schians" were decorated and masked to imitate the heads of buffalo, red deer, and antelope, with the horns, mouths, and nostrils trimmed with red cloth.

At their center was the "first great war chief of the Schians," mounted on a beautiful black stallion. Giving his mount free rein, the Cheyenne war chief galloped full speed up to the Gros Ventre chief, who carried a large American flag, embraced him and others from horseback, and then rode on down the line of marchers shaking hands with selected persons. The war chief was dressed in a blue Spanish coat shirt and a coarse striped blanket, also of Spanish origin, indicating that the Cheyennes had also had contact with traders from Mexico.

The Cheyenne leader, an affable and agreeable man, was very agile and adroit in handling his horse. When he had completed his ceremonial maneuver of embracing the Gros Ventre flag, his companions galloped forward, each selecting a member of the trading caravan to embrace and adopt as a traveling mate during the remainder of the journey to the Cheyenne village. The amity between the previously warring tribes quickly faded, however, when twelve Assiniboins, inveterate enemies of the Cheyennes, appeared in camp and were given haven by the Gros Ventres. The preparations that were being made for Le Borgne to adopt a Cheyenne boy were brought to a sudden standstill by the infuriated Cheyennes. After a serious confrontation that nearly broke out in violence, the trading party left the camp of the hosts.[6]

Between 1806 and 1825 little is known of the Cheyennes or their chiefs. Henry indicates that they had already begun to range southward to the headwaters of the Arkansas and South Platte rivers:

> They generally pass the winter S. of the Black hills, about 20 encampments hence, which I suppose may be 80 or 100 leagues. Here, they say is the source of two large rivers; one runs to the N.E. and the other to the S.; the former falls into the Missourie, below the Pawnee village, I believe, under the name of the Rivière Platte; the other, of course, into the Gulf of Mexico.[7]

Englishman John Bradbury saw a group of Cheyennes on the Missouri River at the Arikara villages in 1811, noting their trading activities to the south. In 1812 trader Joseph Philibert found a large number of Arapahoes, with whom the Cheyennes were known to be associated, on the Arkansas River.

Evidently, during the period that followed, the Cheyennes split after a tribal dispute, and some of them moved south to join the Arapahoes. The Stephen Long expedition met a Cheyenne band on the Arkansas in 1820 and a member of the expedition, Dr. Say, stated that the Cheyennes had seceded from their nation on the north and had come south to place themselves under the protection of the Arapahoes. Say also mentioned another Cheyenne chief who was at the head of a group just returned from the headwaters of the Red River:

> All the Shiennes forthwith left us, in compliance with the preemptory orders of their chief, who seemed to be a man born to commmand, and to be endowed with a spirit of unconquerable ferocity, and capable of inflicting exemplary punishment upon any one who should dare to disobey his orders. He was tall and graceful, with a highly-ridged aquiline nose, corrugated forehead, mouth with corners drawn downward, and rather small, but remarkably piercing eye, which when fixed upon your countenance, appeared strained in the intenseness of its gaze, and to seek rather for the movements of the soul within, than to ascertain the mere lineaments it contemplated. The other chiefs seemed to possess only the dignity of office, without the power of command; the results, probably, of a deficiency of that native energy with which their companion was so pre-eminently endowed.[8]

Dr. Say did not provide the name of the chief, again for lack of anyone to translate the Cheyenne tongue, though he did mention Bear Tooth, grand chief of the Arapahoes, whose influence extended "over all of the country in which he roves."[9] Say described how the Cheyenne chief, who had made a vow against smoking the pipe again, abstained from smoking during their council. Later, however, the chief found a small piece of paper dropped by the Americans and used it to roll up a small quantity of tobacco "into the form of a segar, after the manner of the Spaniards, and thus contented himself with infringing the spirit of his vow, whilst he obeyed it to the letter."[10]

Moving on downstream into present Kansas, the Long expedition met another band of Cheyennes, a war party returning from a raid against the Pawnees on the Platte River. Say was impressed with one of them, whom he identified as Partizan, a "tall,

High-Backed Wolf, or "Wolf on the Hill," as painted by George Catlin on the Teton River in 1832. Catlin described him as "one of the finest looking and most dignified men that I have met in the Indian country, and from the account given of him by the Traders, a man of honour and strictest integrity." *Courtesy of National Collection of Fine Arts, Smithsonian Institution.*

athletic figure" who was painted black with charcoal over all the visible portion of his body.

The main group of the Cheyennes was still located in the vicinity of the Missouri River, however. In the spring of 1825, General Henry Atkinson led a small flotilla of nine keelboats up the Missouri, making treaties with the wild tribes along the river in order to protect the important fur trade which had developed in the wake of Lewis and Clark. On the Fourth of July, Atkinson and Major Benjamin O'Fallon held a council with the Cheyennes and Sioux at the mouth of the Teton River. Here they met High-Backed Wolf,[11] the principal chief of the Cheyennes during the last years before the degenerating influence of the white man's civilization upon the tribe and the first Cheyenne chief about whom something is known.

The whites were entertained with a feast of thirteen dogs well boiled in water brought up from the river in buffalo bags. After feasting and smoking the pipe with the Indian hosts, the Americans were presented the pipe and made a present of the buffalo robes upon which they were then seated. On the following morning the military brigade was reviewed to impress the Indians, its two field pieces being drawn across the plains at full speed, leaving the Indians awestricken. That evening some twenty rockets were thrown up across the wide stream of the Missouri, followed by six shells from the howitzers. The shells "exploded handsomely and made a deep impression upon these savages." Later High-Backed Wolf came into camp leading a handsome mule and presented it along with a Spanish saddle to General Atkinson.[12]

After treating with the Indians, Atkinson and O'Fallon persuaded the Cheyennes to sign a friendship treaty with the United States. By the Treaty of 1825 the government agreed to "receive the Cheyenne tribe of Indians into their friendship and under their protection," to accommodate the Cheyennes with such articles of merchandise as their needs demanded, and to extend to them from time to time "such benefits and acts of kindness as may be convenient." The United States agreed also to establish trading relations with the Cheyenne Nation.[13]

In return the Cheyennes acknowledged that they resided within the territorial limits of the United States and agreed to protect traders sent among them, to deliver up to the authorities any Indian guilty of misconduct, and never to trade guns, ammunition, or other implements of war with any other nation or tribe. Signing the treaty for the Cheyennes were chiefs "Wolf with the High Back," Little Moon, Buffalo Head, and One Who Walks Against the Others, plus seven Cheyenne warriors.

An officer who accompanied the Atkinson expedition was greatly impressed with the dignity and bearing of the Cheyennes. When the Cheyennes were met at the mouth of the Little Teton, the officer wrote home to describe them as the finest and wildest looking Indians they had yet seen:

> They are the genuine children of nature, they have unlike other Indians, all the virtues that nature can give, without the vices of civilization. These must be the men described by Rousseau, when he gained the medal from the Royal Academy in France. They are artless, fearless, and live in constant exercise of moral and Christian virtues, though they know it not.[14]

The journalist of the expedition was highly impressed with the High-Backed Wolf, describing him as "one of the most dignified and elegant looking men I ever saw."

This description of the Cheyenne chieftain was echoed several years later by the western artist George Catlin. During Catlin's visit to a Sioux camp on the Teton River in 1832, the camp was visited by a Cheyenne chief named "Wolf on the Hill" (Nee-hee-o-ee-woo-tis), as the artist gave it, and his comely wife "She Who Bathes Her Knees" (Tis-see-woo-na-tis). Catlin painted both the chief and his wife. His portrait of "Wolf on the Hill" shows him wearing a handsome dress of deerskin, neatly garnished with bands of porcupine-quill work down his shirt sleeves and further fringed with scalp locks. His wife wore a dress of mountain sheepskin decorated with quills and beads. Catlin found the Cheyennes to be superior in physical development. "There is no finer race of men than these in North America," he wrote, "and none superior in stature, excepting the Osages; scarely a man in the tribe, full grown, who is less than six feet in height."[15] Catlin considered "Wolf on the Hill" to be one of the noblest and most dignified Indians he met. The traders confirmed that opinion, saying the Cheyenne chief was a man of high honor and strict integrity.

Only two years after Catlin's meeting with High-Backed Wolf, the chief was killed in a tribal argument.[16] His death in 1834 coincided historically with the opening of Bent's Fort on the Arkansas River, an event that initiated the period of the fur trader among the Cheyennes. With the fur trader came the white man's goods, including whisky and other spirits which greatly demoralized the entire structure of Cheyenne society at a time when the tribe was virtually leaderless.

In 1835, when the exploring expedition of Colonel Henry Dodge visited a Cheyenne encampment near Bent's Fort, the white men found a repulsive sight.[17] Virtually the entire village—men, women, and children—were drunk. The chief's lodge, a very large one, was crowded full of naked people, who surrounded a large keg of whisky at the center of the lodge. The spirits had been obtained from Mexican traders at Taos. The Indians were filling bowls and horn spoons freely with the whisky. Already some of them were reeling about, falling down and staggering back up again, yelling wildly and making demoniac gestures, some frothing at the mouth and so inebriated that they were insensible. Only a few squaws remained sober, as a protection for the rest, but they were enjoying the sport of seeing the others in their drunken state. Lieutenant Gaines P. Kingsbury, the official journalist of the expedition, reported in his chronicle that the Cheyennes "are very fond of whiskey; and will sell their horses, blankets, and everything else they possess for a drink of it. In arranging the goods of this world in the order of rank, they say that whiskey should stand first, then tobacco, third, guns, fourth, horses, and fifth, women."[18]

In a speech to the Dodge expedition, Chief Little Moon, second signer of the Treaty of 1825, reaffirmed that the Cheyennes were remaining true to their pledge of friendship with the whites:

My father, I believe it was my great father, the President, who sent you here to talk to us to-day, and we are glad to see you; we saw troops once before on the Missouri, and took them by the hand; you have been telling us to hold the whites by the hand; we listen to what you say; you wish us to be at peace with all nations; the Crows have been killing our people; I know but little; what you say is very good; your heart is open; one of our parties has gone to the Comanches, another against the Pawnees and Arickaras; my heart is with them; wait until our war parties return; perhaps some of them will be killed.... my heart is glad to see

25

you; I have nothing more to say; I know but little; what I do know
I have told you.[19]

After distributing presents among the Indians, the Americans
marched on down the Arkansas River some fifty miles, where
they encountered another Cheyenne camp of about fifty lodges.
Dodge requested that this village also select a chief from among
their band. The Cheyennes pointed to five men sitting together,
saying they were the principal men; but they were reluctant to
choose among them. Finally one of them was led forward,
whereupon Dodge presented him a letter saying he had been
made a chief. The Cheyennes appropriately named him the
White Man's Chief. Colonel Dodge and his men marched on
down the Arkansas River, and the Cheyennes returned to their
way of life on the prairie.

High-Backed Wolf and the other chiefs had welcomed the
white man and his trade goods. Though the Cheyennes did not
yet realize it, in the years ahead they and the chiefs who led them
would be forced to consider a new way of existence in the face of
the white man's civilization, which was spreading rapidly across
the plains toward them.

3

Chiefs of the South

Yellow Wolf, Old Tobacco, Slim Face

*Tell our great father that the Cheyennes are ready and
willing to obey him in everything; but, in settling
down and raising corn, that is a thing which we know
nothing about.*

Yellow Wolf

Yellow Wolf[1] played a prominent role as a warrior, chief, and
tribal elder from the mid-1820's until he was killed at Sand
Creek in 1864. As one of the early principal chiefs of the Southern
Cheyennes during American exploration and expansion in
the mid–nineteenth century, he, like High-Backed Wolf, sought
to keep the Cheyenne Nation at peace with the whites. He once
asked that a fort be built for the Cheyennes as a place where his
people could cultivate the ground and raise corn as they had in
times past. But even Yellow Wolf miscalculated the intensity of
the Cheyenne war culture. It had led the once-oppressed
Cheyennes to great power and prestige and had become the
essential fiber of Cheyenne manhood. In the face of American
intrusion onto the central plains, the Cheyenne war societies
would ultimately wrest the tribal leadership from the control of
the peace chiefs and determine the destiny of the Cheyenne
Nation.

A small, wiry man of high intelligence, Yellow Wolf is credited
with being at the head of the Cheyenne war party that first
met the Bents and Céran St. Vrain on the Arkansas River
around 1824 or 1826. According to accounts given by Porcupine
Bull in later years, the Cheyennes were then returning
from the Red River country of Texas with a large herd of stolen
Comanche horses and stopped at the Bent stockade on Fountain
River in present Colorado. Yellow Wolf told the American traders
that the stockade was too near the mountains, that in winter
the Indians could not range so far away from the plains where

27

the buffalo were. He promised that his Hairy Rope (Hévataneo) band would move down and trade with the white men if they would build their fort farther down the Arkansas River. The Bent and St. Vrain Company agreed, and Fort William, or Bent's Fort, was constructed at the mouth of the Purgatoire River in the early 1830's.[2]

The establishment of Bent's Fort and trading operations solidified the move southward of the bands that ultimately became known as the Southern Cheyennes, Yellow Wolf's band among them. In migrating south, the Cheyennes came into closer contact with the Comanche and Kiowa range between the Arkansas and Red rivers. The hugh horse herds of these tribes were tempting prey for Cheyenne raiding parties; Yellow Wolf's Hairy Rope band was especially active in raids on the Comanche and Kiowa herds.

On one occasion, in 1829, the Comanches under Chief Bull Hump came north and crossed the Arkansas River in an effort to regain a large herd of horses that the Cheyennes had taken. Finding the Cheyennes encamped on the South Platte River, they raided their horse herds and stole back the Comanche horses plus some belonging to the Cheyennes. Bull Hump then retreated quickly to the Arkansas River where, believing he was safe, he went into camp. But Yellow Wolf happened to be on the Arkansas at the time with a large party chasing wild mustangs. Discovering Bull Hump's camp, Yellow Wolf struck at dawn and stampeded the horse herd. When the Comanches gave chase, a fight ensued. The Cheyennes, however, were armed with guns, while the Comanches had only bows and arrows, and Yellow Wolf escaped with the thrice-stolen horses as well as some Comanche scalps.[3]

Accounts of the Colonel Henry Dodge expedition of 1835 are noticeably absent of any mention of Yellow Wolf. Quite possibly he was away from the Arkansas River with one of the raiding parties mentioned by the chronicler of the expedition, Lieutenant Kingsbury, either to the Red River or in the north against the Pawnees. Yellow Wolf's prominence with the tribe during this period is indicated by a letter William Bent wrote in 1838. Bent asked the United States government to send out the medals that Dodge had promised for chiefs Walking Whirlwind, White Cow, and Yellow Wolf.[4]

Yellow Wolf, as sketched by Lieutenant Janes W. Abert at Bent's Fort in 1845. Abert said, "He is a man of considerable influence, of enlarged views, and gifted with more foresight than any other man in his tribe." *Courtesy of Western History Collections, University of Oklahoma Library.*

The horse-stealing raids and warfare between the Cheyennes and Arapahoes on the one hand and the allied Comanche and Kiowa tribes on the other continued for several years. In 1836 another clash between Yellow Wolf and Bull Hump reportedly took place. The Cheyenne leader directed a raid that took another large Comanche horse herd from the North Fork of the Red River. Bull Hump again followed with a large party of warriors, tracking Yellow Wolf's band to Bent's Fort. George Bent recalled that, before going on, Yellow Wolf had presented one of the horses to William Bent, and fortunately the animal was hidden inside the fort when Bull Hump passed by. The horse was named Yellow Wolf in honor of the Cheyenne chief, and it became an excellent hunting horse for a Bent trader named Kit Carson.[5]

The following year, 1837, a party of forty-eight Cheyenne Bowstring society soldiers were caught afoot by Kiowas and Comanches on the North Fork of the Red River while making a raid on the Kiowa horse herds. They were killed to the man and scalped. When the Cheyennes learned of the fate of the Bowstrings some time later, Yellow Wolf and the warrior leaders vowed to avenge their deaths by attacking their enemies and taking no one alive. They were joined by their allies, the Arapahoes.[6]

Camping on the Arkansas near present Dodge City, Kansas, the two tribes sent out scouts who spotted a small war party of Kiowas on Wolf Creek of northwestern Oklahoma. This news was reported back to the main village of Cheyennes and Arapahoes, which had been moving southward to Beaver Creek. Beaver Creek joins with Wolf Creek to form the North Canadian River. A large force of Cheyenne and Arapaho warriors, led in part by Yellow Wolf, crossed the high divide between the two creeks and located an encampment of Kiowas, Comanches, and Plains Apaches. The warriors attacked the camp, and both sides lost important chiefs and warriors in the battle before the Cheyennes and Arapahoes withdrew.

Though the fight was inconclusive militarily, it convinced each side of the other's strength and led to the great peace council of 1840. The five tribes met near Bent's Fort, the Comanches returning the scalps of the Bowstring soldiers and the Kiowas giving the Cheyennes and Arapahoes many horses. The Cheyennes in return made gifts of their trade goods—guns, blankets, calico, beads, brass kettles, and American foodstuff such as dried apples, cornmeal, coffee, and sugar. This peace agreement established an amity which, though sometimes shaky, maintained permanently peaceful relations.[7]

Peace had been made with the Kiowas and Comanches, but the Cheyennes continued a persistent tribal warfare with the Pawnees of southern Nebraska and the Utes of northwestern Colorado. In 1844 trouble erupted with the Delawares of eastern Kansas. On a spring day a party of Delaware trappers and hunters were returning across the plains from a trip to the Rocky Mountains. They encountered a Cheyenne family and chased them back to their village on the Arickaree Fork of the Republican River. Immediately the braves of the village mounted their horses and rode out to fight. Yellow Wolf restrained the Cheyenne warriors, pointing out that they were not at war with the Delawares and should try to make peace.[8]

The Delawares would not listen to the Cheyenne peace attempts and kept firing whenever the Cheyennes rode toward them. Finally the Cheyennes charged the Delawares and killed them all, acquiring a large number of animal skins from the massacred hunting party. Lieutenant John Frémont, returning from California, passed along the Arkansas River shortly after the fight. On July 5, 1844, his party met a large village of Cheyennes, Sioux, and Arapahoes twenty miles east of Bent's Fort. He reported that "a few days previous they had massacred a party of fifteen Delawares, whom they had discovered in a fort on the Smoky Hill river, losing in the affair several of their own people. They were desirous that we should bear a pacific message to the Delawares on the frontier, from whom they expected retaliation."[9]

Breaking up into different bands, the Cheyennes scattered. Yellow Wolf and Old Tobacco took their people southward to the Cimarron River.[10] They were back on the Arkansas River the following year, however, when Frémont returned. He was accompanied by some Delawares to whom he had delivered the Cheyennes' message. The Cheyenne leaders apologized and were presented with a medicine pipe by the Delaware chief.[11]

With Frémont was Lieutenant James W. Abert, who was assigned to lead an exploring party to the South Canadian River and eastward along it to Fort Gibson. Abert sketched a number of the Indians at Bent's Fort, including Yellow Wolf, "head chief of the Cheyenne Nation," who consented to sit for him. Abert drew a side view of the chief with a pencil. But when Yellow Wolf saw that others of his tribe were done in color, he was very dissatisfied and accused Abert of representing him badly. The officer finally convinced the Cheyenne leader that the pencil sketch was incomplete and would be improved later, and Yellow Wolf went away apparently satisfied.[12]

A year later, in 1846, Lieutenant Abert was at Bent's Fort once again, this time with Colonel Stephen Watts Kearny's Army of the West on its way to invade New Mexico. But Abert became ill and was left behind at the fort, giving him the opportunity to know Yellow Wolf better. He found the Cheyenne leader to be far more than a simple warrior:

> He is a man of considerable influence, of enlarged views, and gifted with more foresight than any other man in his tribe. He frequently talks of the diminishing number of his people, and the decrease of the once abundant buffalo. He says that in a few years they will become extinct; and unless the Indians wish to pass away also, they will have to adopt the habits of the white people, using such measures to produce subsistence as will render them independent of the precarious reliance afforded by the game.[13]

Yellow Wolf was so serious about the matter that he offered to pay John Simpson Smith, trader and interpreter at Bent's Fort, in mules if he would build the Cheyennes a fort of their own and teach them to cultivate the ground on lands set aside for them by the government and to raise cattle in the fashion of the whites. Two years later, when the first agent for the Cheyennes, Thomas Fitzpatrick, conferred with the Cheyennes at Bent's Fort, Yellow Wolf made a speech, again showing his farsighted awareness of the problems faced by his people:

> My father, we are very poor and ignorant, even like the wolves in the prairie; we are not endowed with the wisdom of the white people. Father, this day we rejoice; we are no more poor and wretched; our great father has at length condescended to notice us, poor and wretched as we are; father, we have not been warring against your people; why should we? On the contrary, if our great father wishes our aid, the Cheyenne warriors shall be ready at a moment's warning to assist in punishing those bad people, the Comanches. . . .
>
> Tell our great father that the Cheyennes are ready and willing to obey him in every thing; but, in settling down and raising corn, that is a thing which we know nothing about, and if he will send some of his people to learn us, we will at once commence, and make every effort to live like the whites. We have long since

noticed the decrease of the buffalo, and are well aware it cannot last much longer.[14]

Even more intimate contact with Yellow Wolf had been made the previous winter when Lewis H. Garrard, a young Cincinnatian, visited Bent's Fort and spent some time in the Cheyenne camps with John Smith. Garrard first mentioned Yellow Wolf's village as being located at the "Buttes," a day's ride away. Yellow Wolf, the famous horse-stealer of former days, Garrard reported, had just lost forty of his best animals to a Pawnee war party.[15]

Later Garrard had the occasion to meet Yellow Wolf personally when the Cheyenne principal chief visited Smith for a few days. Garrard told of an occasion when Yellow Wolf and Smith were seated at the lodge fire on a cold winter's day, talking. Suddenly a kettle on the fire boiled over. The Cheyenne reacted immediately, deliberately laying down the pipe he was about to smoke and covering his head with his robe. He then bowed to the ground and remained so for several minutes. When he arose "his countenance wore a resigned, though sad aspect, as one engaged in spiritual devotion."[16]

An Englishman, Captain George F. Ruxton, passed along the Arkansas River during the summer of 1847 and also met Yellow Wolf. Ruxton described Yellow Wolf's lodge, located in the center of the Cheyenne encampment, as follows:

> The skin of it was dyed a conspicuous red. Before the lodges of each of the principal chiefs and warriors was a stack of spears, from which hung his shield and arms; whilst the skins of the lodge itself were covered with devices and hieroglyphics, describing his warlike achievements. Before one was a painted pole supporting several smoke-dried scalps, which dangled in the wind, rattling against the post like bags of peas.[17]

Of Yellow Wolf himself, Ruxton wrote:

> Now O-cun-no-whurst, the Yellow Wolf, grand chief of the Shian, complains of certain grave offences against the dignity of his nation! A trader from the "big lodge" (the fort) has been in his village, and before the trade was opened, in laying the customary chief's gift "on the prairie" has not "opened his hand" but "squeezed out his present between his fingers" grudgingly and with too sparing measure. This was hard to bear, but the Yellow Wolf would say no more![18]

OLD TOBACCO

During his sojourn on the Arkansas River with Smith, Garrard had also been a guest in the lodge of Old Tobacco, whose tipi was often used by William Bent to house trade goods when he visited the Cheyenne camps. "We pulled off our saddles in front of Se-ne-mone's or 'Tobacco's' lodge," Garrard wrote. "Our host was afflicted with sore eyes; but we were welcomed to the 'back part,' in true feeling of hospitality."[19]

When Thomas Fitzpatrick made his first call on the Cheyennes as their agent in the fall of 1847, Yellow Wolf informed him that only a short time before "one of our wisest and best chiefs" had been killed by the white people. It was Old Tobacco. Known as Cinemo by some whites, he had always been considered a "good Indian" and was very friendly to all Americans. He and his band had just returned from below the Arkansas River when he discovered a wagon train on the Santa Fe road. Knowing that a well-armed and dangerous Comanche war party was in the area, he decided to warn the whites. But upon reaching the camp of the wagon train, he was fired upon and mortally wounded. Before he died, five days later, he told his family and tribal members not to avenge his death. He had been killed by his white friends, he said, who had not known who he was.[20]

William Boggs, a frontiersman of the period, said that when Cinemo had approached the government wagon train, a teamster guard had waved his hand for the chief to "Go back. Go back." But the signal was very similar to a sign language gesture, raising the hand at arm's length and bringing it down, meaning "Come to me." Old Tobacco ran toward the teamster and was shot down.[21]

SLIM FACE

Another Cheyenne chief who was active for peace during this period was one the whites knew as Slim Face.[22] In 1844, Slim Face accompanied a Bent and St. Vrain wagon train to Saint Louis. His purpose was twofold: to get the government to stop the sale of ardent spirits to the Indians and to have the killing of buffalo calves by the whites halted. Rufus Sage reported meeting with the Bent's Fort caravan at the Pawnee Fork and seeing Slim Face.[23]

Abert later met the chief after he had returned to Bent's Fort. Slim Face was not only a great warrior and a much-chosen partisan for war parties but also a keen observer. He closely scrutinized things he saw and remembered them in detail. All this made him a man of much influence, and tribal audiences listened intently to his stories. Thus his narrations of his experiences in Saint Louis were heard with no one daring to utter a word of doubt.

He told the others of his tribe about attending a circus one evening, recollecting in extraordinary detail the color, the markings, and the trappings of every horse that appeared. It seemed almost incomprehensible to him that white men could ride so well. In fact, horseback riding was the only superiority that Slim Face acknowledged for civilization. He also could not understand how so many people could live together in one village, so far from any hunting grounds. Intrigued with the number of people living in Saint Louis, he decided to count them himself. Seating himself on a street corner, Slim Face began notching a stick for each person that passed by. He notched and notched and notched as the multitudes flowed back and forth before him. Soon the stick was virtually notched away, and Slim Face was forced to give up in dismay.[24]

Garrard described a visit to the lodge of Slim Face:

> ... We felt at home. A large wooden bowl of meat was set before us, to which, with coffee, we did ample justice.... In Vip-po-nah's lodge was his grandson, a boy of six or seven months. Every morning, his mother washed him in cold water and sent him out to air to make him hardy; he would come in, perfectly nude, from his airing, about half-frozen. How he would laugh and brighten up as he felt the warmth of the fire! Being a boy, the parents have great hopes of him as a brave and chief (the acme of Indian greatness); his father dotes upon him, holding him in his arms, singing in low tone, and in various ways showing his extreme affection.[25]

Garrard's account is the last heard of Slim Face for two decades. Not until the Treaty of Medicine Lodge in 1867 did his name appear again in records of the Cheyennes, this time as a signer of the treaty. It might be supposed that this was another

Cheyennes taken captive by Custer on the Sweetwater River in the Texas Panhandle in 1869, with Slim Face on far right. This photograph was likely taken by William S. Soule at Camp Supply. *Courtesy of Oklahoma State Historical Society.*

Slim Face were it not for George Bent's claim that one of the three chiefs captured by Custer on the Sweetwater River in 1869 was "Lean Face," whom Bent said was eighty years old when he was killed in a prison fracas at Fort Hays during the summer of 1869.[26]

Following the massacre of Black Kettle's Cheyennes at the Washita River, Sheridan and Custer had moved on to Fort Cobb, where they stayed until the end of 1868. In early January, 1869, they established Fort Sill in present Oklahoma. Later that spring,

Custer conducted a campaign into the Texas Panhandle with the dual purpose of driving the Cheyennes to the reservation and of rescuing two white women held captive by the tribe. While he was being entertained in his camp by the Cheyennes, Custer ordered his officers to take the Cheyenne chiefs prisoner. All but three of the Indians escaped, however. Custer threatened to hang the three chiefs if the two white girls were not released. The Cheyennes released the women, but still Custer refused to free the three Cheyennes. He took them with him to Camp Supply and on to Fort Hays, where other Cheyenne prisoners, all women and children, were being held. At Hays the stockade guard attempted to separate the three men from the compound containing the women without the services of an interpreter. Thinking the men were to be shot, a squaw plunged a knife into the back of a guard, initiating a free-for-all fracas in which one Cheyenne was shot and another, Slim Face, received a bayonet wound through his body, causing his death a few days later.

Thus all three of these peace chiefs were killed by whites: Slim Face at Fort Hays; Old Tobacco as he attempted to warn a government wagon train; and Yellow Wolf, who was shot down on a cold November morning in 1864 at Sand Creek, only a short way from where he had met the Bents some forty years earlier and invited them to build their fort in Cheyenne country.

Old Wolf and Lame White Man, Northern Cheyennes, taken in 1873 during a visit to Washington, D.C. *Courtesy of Smithsonian Institution, Neg. No. 269.*

38

Spotted Wolf and Crazy Head, Northern Cheyennes, at Washington, D.C., 1873. *Courtesy of Smithsonian Institution, Neg. No. 268.*

Arapaho and Cheyenne Delegation

Above: Cheyennes visiting Carlisle, Pennsylvania, 1885. *Seated:* Old Crow, Whirlwind, Big Jake, and Left Hand. *Standing:* Whirlwind's wife, Red Wolf, Yellow Bear, Black Wolf, and Black Wolf's wife. *Courtesy of Oklahoma Publishing Company.*

Facing page, top: Southern Cheyenne delegation at the Annual Grand Council of 1875 at Okmulgee, Indian Territory. *Seated:* Little Chief, Starving Elk, White Shield, and Little Bear. *Standing:* Plenty Horses, interpreter Phil McCusker, and Feathered Wolf. *Courtesy of Smithsonian Institution, Neg. No. 55,475.*

Facing page, bottom: Southern Cheyenne and Arapaho delegation at Washington, D.C., 1880. The Cheyennes are on the left in the photograph. They are Big Horse, Bob-Tail, Man-on-a-Cloud, and Mad Wolf. The Arapahoes are Left Hand (*center*), Little Raven, and Yellow Bear. Agent John D. Miles and Robert Bent stand at far right. *Courtesy of National Archives.*

Southern Cheyenne and Arapaho chiefs visit Oklahoma City shortly after its founding in April, 1889. Present are Southern leaders Little Chief, Cloud Chief, Cut Nose, Starving Elk, and Wolf Face, plus a

number of other frontier notables, including George Bent, John D.
Miles, former Governor of Kansas Samuel Crawford, Left Hand, and
boomer leader William L. Couch. *Courtesy of Edna Couch.*

Above: Chief Whirlwind with his daughter and grandchildren. *Courtesy of El Reno Carnegie Library.*

Facing page, top: Cheyenne and Arapaho delegation at Washington, 1891. Arapahoes, seated: Scabby Bull, Black Coyote, the wife of Left Hand, and Left Hand. Cheyennes, seated: Cloud Chief, Little Chief, Wolf Robe, and Little Bear. Standing: Arapaho chief Row of Lodges, Black Wolf, Jessie Bent, Captain D. L. Wright, Leonard Tyler, Kish Hawkins, and Benjamin Beveridge. *Courtesy of Western History Collections, University of Oklahoma Library.*

Facing page, bottom: Cheyenne and Arapaho delegation at Washington, 1895. *Seated:* Southern Cheyennes Little Wolf, Whirlwind, Little Chief, Cloud Chief, and White Horse. *Standing:* Capt. A. L. Woodson of Fort Reno; Arapaho chiefs Row of Lodges and Left Hand; Robert Burns, Cheyenne; and Clever Warden, Arapaho. *Courtesy of Smithsonian Institution, Neg. no. 50,317.*

Whirlwind in old age with his family. *Courtesy of Western History Collections, University of Oklahoma Library.*

4

The Mid-Century Chiefs

Porcupine Bear, Old Bark, Alights-on-the-Cloud,
Walking Whirlwind

I will go and sit with my fathers in the spirit land,
where I shall soon point down to the last expiring fire
of the Cheyennes, and when they inquire the cause of
this decline of their people, I will tell them with a
straight tongue that it was the fire-water of the trader
that put it out.

Porcupine Bear

There were several important Cheyenne chiefs of the mid-century period. One was Porcupine Bear.[1] James P. Beckwourth (Beckwith), the famous mulatto frontiersman, knew Porcupine Bear on the South Platte River around 1840 and mentioned the Cheyenne chief in the autobiography he wrote in 1856. A speech that he ascribed to the Cheyenne chief undoubtedly was not a verbatim transcription, but it throws added light on the liquor problem faced by the Cheyenne leaders. During an argument with his brother-in-law, Bob-Tailed Horse, over the opening of some kegs of whisky, Porcupine Bear made an eloquent plea against the use of "fire-water" by the Cheyennes:

Once we were a great and powerful nation: our hearts were proud, and our arms were strong. But a few winters ago all other tribes feared us; now the Pawnees dare to cross our hunting grounds, and kill our buffalo. Once we could beat the Crows, and, unaided, destroyed their villages; now we call other villages to our assistance, and we can not defend ourselves from the assaults of the enemy. How is this, Cheyennes: The Crows drink no whiskey. The earnings of their hunters and toils of their women are bartered to the white man for weapons and ammunition. This keeps them powerful and dreaded by their enemies. We kill buffalo by the thousand; our women's hands are sore with dressing the robes; and what do we part with them to the white trader for? We pay them for the white man's fire-water, which turns our brains upside down, which makes our hearts black, renders our arms weak. It takes away our warriors' skill, and makes them shoot wrong in battle. Our enemies, who drink no whiskey, when they shoot, always kill their foe. We have no ammunition to encounter our foes, and we have become as dogs, which have nothing but their teeth.

Our prairies were once covered with horses as the trees are covered with leaves. Where are they now? Ask the Crows, who drink no whiskey. When we are all drunk, they come and take them from before our eyes; our legs are helpless, and we can not follow them. We are only fearful to our women, who take up their children and conceal themselves among the rocks and in the forest, for we are famishing. Our children are now sick, and our women are weak with watching. Let us not scare them away from our lodges, with their sick children in their arms. The Great Spirit will be offended at it. I had rather go to the great and happy hunting-ground now than live and see the downfall of my nation. Our fires begin to burn dim, and will soon go out entirely. My people are becoming like the Pawnees: they buy the whiskey of the trader, and, because he is weak and not able to fight them, they go and steal from his lodge.

I say, let us buy of the Crow [Beckwourth] what is useful and good, but his whiskey we will not touch; let him take that away with him. I have spoken all I have to say, and if my brother wishes to kill me for it, I am ready to die. I will go and sit with my fathers in the spirit land, where I shall soon point down to the last expiring fire of the Cheyennes, and when they inquire the cause of this decline of their people, I will tell them with a straight tongue that it was the fire-water of the trader that put it out.[2]

Porcupine Bear himself, however, was to become a victim of the trader's fire-water. According to Cheyenne tradition, following the slaying of the forty-eight Bowstring soldiers in 1837, it was Porcupine Bear who, as chief of the Dog Soldiers, took up the Cheyenne war pipe and carried it around to the Cheyenne camps in order to gather a war party to seek vengeance against the Kiowas. One village that he went to on the South Platte River had just been sold a large amount of liquor by traders from Fort Laramie.

Visiting in the lodge with some relatives and friends, Porcupine Bear joined the others in getting very drunk. He sat in a corner by himself singing Dog Soldier war songs, while two of his cousins became embroiled in a drunken fight. One of them, Little Creek, was on top of the other, whose name was Around, and was about to stab him to death with a knife. Hearing Around's call for help, Porcupine Bear jumped to his feet in a drunken rage, wrested the knife from Little Creek, and then stabbed him several times. He then made Around use the knife and help finish off Little Creek.[3]

As a result of this act of murder, the Cheyennes outlawed Porcupine Bear and all of his relations. Yellow Wolf took over the honor of carrying the war pipe, reformed the practically depleted Bowstring society, and assigned that war society the task of moving the sacred Medicine Arrows against the Kiowas. Porcupine Bear and the Dog Soldiers did participate in the Wolf Creek battle against the Kiowas and Comanches, even though they were forced to camp apart from the other Cheyennes. Porcupine Bear's band supposedly counted the first coups in the fight, the chief himself killing twelve Kiowas. They were not accorded the honor, however, because of their having been outlawed by the main body of the Cheyennes.[4] It was Porcupine Bear's banishment that changed the Dog Soldiers from a society of warriors to an outlawed tribal division.[5]

The only historical record we have of Porcupine Bear was at the Fort Laramie treaty council in 1851. He was mentioned at one point by the two newspapermen who covered the treaty for the *Missouri Republican*. At the outset of the council, a war party of young Cheyennes killed and scalped two young Snake Indians, whose tribe was also attending the council. A meeting was held by the commissioners in an effort to calm the potentially dangerous situation. After considerable time had been consumed in the customary smoking of the pipe, Porcupine Bear was first to rise to his feet and make a speech.

He addressed himself principally to his young men, urging them to treat the Snakes as friends, to smoke with them, take them by the hands, and give them presents. The reporters described the chief as "peculiarly forcible, judging from his gestures and the translation of his speech by the interpreter."[6] Porcupine Bear urged the young men to listen to the counsel of the elders and in the future not to go to war or act without the permission of the chiefs.

After several speeches by other chiefs, the Cheyennes presented the Snakes with presents of blankets, bolts of scarlet cloth, knives, tobacco, and other goods. Then they returned the scalps of the two Snakes they had killed. The two correspondents do not again mention Porcupine Bear, and it is perhaps significant that he was not one of the four Cheyenne chiefs who signed the Treaty of Fort Laramie.[7]

OLD BARK

Old Bark, or Bear's Feather,[8] was one of the four Cheyenne chiefs to sign the 1851 treaty and the amended version of the treaty on the South Platte River on August 31, 1853.[9] Jim Beckwourth got to know Old Bark around Fort St. Vrain in the early 1840's, and in his autobiography he referred to the chief as the "patriarch of the Cheyennes." Beckwourth told how once the chief had requested his help in disposing of two kegs of whisky that had been brought to his village.[10]

Lieutenant James W. Abert met Old Bark at Bent's Fort on the Arkansas River in 1845, describing him as "second in rank to 'Yellow Wolf,' and . . . remarkable for perseverance, enterprise, and bravery; although now very old, yet about a year since he went as far as the settlements on a war trail. He regretted much that he had not a robe for me emblazoned with the history of his bold achievements, but unfortunately he had given them all away."[11]

With Abert's party was a group of Delaware Indians who presented the Cheyennes with a peace pipe to reconcile the differences between the two tribes as the Cheyennes had requested through Frémont the year before. During a council Yellow Wolf said a few words to the Delawares, and then Old Bark followed with a speech:

> We have been in great dread lest you should make war upon us, and, although our women and children have been suffering for food, were afraid to venture forth, for we are now weak and poor, and our ground diminished to a small circle. The whites have been amongst us, and destroyed our buffalo, antelope, and deer, and have cut down our timber; but we are so desirous to keep peaceful that we take no notice of it, for we regard the Delawares and whites as one people. My heart is now exceedingly glad, and we feel as if the whole sky had been lifted up to a great height. I never wished to see the prairie deluged with blood, and was glad when I beheld this pipe, which I shall always reverence as great medicine. It shall be handed down to our children as a memorial of this day,

when we re-established our firm friendship with our brothers towards the rising sun. I have at my village a fine horse which I will give you.[12]

Garrard also met the chief on the Arkansas River during the winter of 1846–47, telling how he witnessed a war dance in a Cheyenne camp: "Thirty of the chiefs and principal men were ranged by the pile of blazing logs. By their invitation, I sat down near 'Old Bark,' and smoked death and its concomitant train of evils to those audacious tribes who doubted the courage or supremacy of the brave, the great, and powerful Cheyenne Nation."[13]

At Fort Laramie Old Bark made a speech to the treaty council:

> Grand Father and Father: I am glad to see so many Indians and whites meeting in peace. It makes my heart glad, and I shall be more happy at home. I am glad you have taken pity on us, and come to see us. The buffalo used to be plenty in our country, but it is getting scarce. We got enough to come here and keep us a while, but our meat will not last long. As the sun looks down upon us—(so) the Great Spirit sees me I am willing, Grand Father, to do as you tell me to do. I know you will tell me right, and that it will be good for me and my people. We regard this as a great *medicine day,* when our pipe and water shall be one, and we all shall be at peace. Our young men, Grand Father, whom you want to go with you to the States, are ready, and they shall go. I shall look to their return when the grass begins to grow again. If all the nations here were willing to do what you tell them, and do what they say as we are, then we could sleep in peace; we would not have to watch our horses or our lodges in the night.[14]

George Bent told a story concerning Bark, or Bear's Feather, as a young warrior. Having gone to steal horses from a Pawnee camp, Bear's Feather was captured by the chief of the village. The Pawnee chief had his wife feed the Cheyenne and later gave him a fine white mule with a silver-mounted Mexican saddle to ride home on. But when he reached his village, Bark told his people that he had stolen the mule and saddle. Everyone had considered him to be very brave for the exploit, but when the truth was later learned he was not thought of so highly.[15]

It is not impossible that the Old Bark whom Abert and Garrard met and who signed the Treaty of Fort Laramie in 1851 was the same Old Bark whom Henry C. Keeling knew around 1879 in Indian Territory. Keeling, after learning the Cheyenne language while serving with General Nelson A. Miles in building Fort Keogh on the Tongue River following Custer's massacre on the Little Bighorn, was assigned as post trader at Cantonment in Indian Territory. He told how one day, as a foolish prank, he pinned a newspaper to the blanket of an old Indian named Old Bark and set it afire. Old Bark was very angry and told the old warriors that he was going to kill Keeling.

Then one day while visiting a Cheyenne camp on the North Fork of the Canadian River, Keeling was fired upon from some timber along the river, the ball taking leather off Keeling's saddle pommel. The trader felt certain that it was Old Bark who had given him the close call. On another occasion Keeling and two army officer friends entered a Cheyenne camp to witness a dance. They entered a lodge and discovered that Old Bark was present. When the pipe was passed around, Keeling refused it on the grounds that Old Bark had threatened to kill him.

Old Bark immediately jumped to his feet at the insult of having the pipe refused and commenced "counting his queue," promising again to kill Keeling just as soon as he could go to his lodge and get his gun. After Old Bark had stormed out, another Cheyenne gave Keeling a pistol and told him and his two friends to make a run for it. "And I believe that we three men never made a better run than we did that evening," Keeling commented.

But the story of Old Bark and Keeling eventually came to a happy ending. Keeling happened to discover the old chief where he had been thrown by his horse on the South Canadian River. The old man's leg was broken. Keeling carried Old Bark back to the post and had his leg set by the post surgeon. The two men thereafter became close friends.[16]

ALIGHTS-ON-THE-CLOUD

Alights-on-the-Cloud[17] was a chief of the Cheyennes at the time of the Fort Laramie council. Moreover, he was one of the three Cheyennes who accompanied the commissioners to Washington, D.C., after the council. Though there was later another Cheyenne named Touching Cloud, the absence of the name of the earlier chief from the records for a long period following 1851 indicates the validity of the claim that Alights-on-the-Cloud was killed in a battle with the Pawnees in 1852.[18]

Cheyenne accounts tell of how Alights-on-the-Cloud took part in the fight with the Delawares in 1844 wearing a suit of armor given to him by his father, Medicine Water. The armor had been traded from a Mexican trader. Alights-on-the-Cloud wore the armor under his blanket and advanced on the Delawares to draw their fire. When the Delawares had discharged their muzzle-loaders, the other Cheyennes charged and caught them with their guns empty.[19]

Alights-on-the-Cloud was a very handsome man and was considered to be kindhearted as well as brave.[20] He was the first man chosen from the Cheyennes to go with the commissioners to visit the Great Father in Washington along with White Antelope and Little Chief and a number of men from the other tribes at the council. On the second of October, the party of commissioners, interpreters, and chiefs arrived at Fort Kearny on the Platte River. There a council was held with some twenty Pawnee chiefs and braves, historic enemies of the Cheyennes.

Big Fatty of the Pawnees made a speech in which he expressed a desire for peace with the Cheyennes. Though several of the other Indians smoked the peace pipe with Big Fatty and made friendship speeches of their own, Alights-on-the-Cloud refused the pipe when it came his turn. He was not angry with the Pawnees, he said, but he could not betray his host and talk peace when even at the moment there might well be a Cheyenne war party on its way to a Pawnee village.[21]

The arrival of the delegation in Saint Louis on the way to Washington, D.C., was reported by the *Missouri Republican*. The news account listed the Indians by name and described the reaction of Alights-on-the-Cloud and the others to the trip:

> The journey to the Indians, since their arrival in the settlement, has been one of great wonder, and in some cases of alarm and fear. Except what they had seen at Fort Laramie and Fort Kearny, they know nothing of the *white man's lodge,* but their greatest astonishment was in seeing a steamboat, and their fears were excessive upon going upon it. They called it the fire horse, and it was a considerable time before they could reconcile themselves to "the noise and confusion" of blowing off steam, the steam whistle,

White Antelope, Alights-on-the-Cloud, and the earlier Little Chief and during their visit to Washington, D.C., in 1851. They were the first of their tribe who dared to visit the Great Father. *Courtesy of Smithsonian Institution, Bureau of American Ethnology Collection, Neg. no. 240-a.*

ringing the bell, &c. At first the motion of the boat made some of them sick; but they are among the most intelligent of their respective tribes, and in time became reconciled and quieted. They were highly delighted when they saw the "fire horse's *brother* (another steamboat) with a papoose" (the yaw!) hitched to the tail, ascending the river. Thus far, as soon as their apprehensions of danger had diminished, they became quite inquisitive and highly delighted with everything they met with.[22]

There were other amazements for the Indians in the nation's capital. They were taken on tours about the city in carriages, shown military forts, the naval yards, and the arsenal, and escorted to the White House to meet with the Great Father, President Millard Fillmore, Most amazing to all was the Central Market, where hung rows on rows of both domestic and wild fowl. One of the chiefs refurnished his war bonnet with feathers from the wing of a large turkey. On one occasion they were taken to a hotel to meet the exiled Hungarian patriot Louis Kossuth. Finally, in late January, 1852, the Indians were escorted back to their homes on the plains and in the mountains.[23]

President Fillmore had urged the wild Indians to turn to agriculture and remain at peace with their neighbors. Alights-on-the-Cloud and the others were impressed; still in less than half a year after his return to the plains, apparently, the Cheyenne chief was dead at the hands of the Pawnees. During the summer of 1852 a very large war party, consisting of 230 Cheyennes plus Arapahoes, Sioux, Apaches, and Kiowas, went out against a big Pawnee encampment that was holding its summer buffalo hunt on the Beaver River of Kansas. Alights-on-the-Cloud was wearing his famous shirt of armor. A Pawnee Indian, Eagle Chief, gave the following description of Alights-on-the-Cloud's part in the fight:

He rode one of the largest horses they [the Pawnees] had ever seen, a roan horse, and in his hand he held a saber. I, myself, was standing near the west end of the line and, looking over, saw the man coming from the east end, holding up the saber in his hand, riding down the front of the line going toward the west. He rode close to where the Pawnees were, and as he passed them, they gave back a little. When he reached the end of the Pawnee line, this man did not go back the way he had come, but went around on the other side, where his own people were, and went along in front of that line very slowly; and when he came to the other end of it, he turned and made another charge in front of the Pawnee line, just as he had done before. He had nothing wrapped around him. He could not bend over, but sat straight up on his horse. His head was round and partly covered up with this iron, so that his hair could not be seen.

When he made the first charge down the line he did not try to run over people. The second time he started to make a charge as he had done before. As he was coming down the line the second time all the Pawnees on the east end made backward movement, because this terrible man was coming.

There was one man, however, a warrior named Carrying the

Shield in Front, Ta wi ta da hi la sa, who did not move back. He stood there in the same place. Iron Shirt came toward him, thinking that he was going to kill Carrying the Shield in Front. Just as he came quite close to him Iron Shirt raised his hand in which he held the saber, but just as he reached down to hit the Pawnee, Carrying the Shield in Front shot him with an arrow, and it struck Iron Shirt in the eye, and he fell off his horse in front of the Pawnee.[24]

WALKING WHIRLWIND

Walking Whirlwind[25] had been one of those selected as a chief during Colonel Henry Dodge's visit to the Arkansas River in 1835, and indications are that he was an important man among the Cheyennes for a number of years. He was one of the three Cheyenne chiefs for whom William Bent wrote the letter in 1838 requesting the promised medals from the government. Rufus Sage, who visited the Rocky Mountains and central plains regions during the early 1840's, mentioned that during the winter of 1843–44 an Indian named Whirlwind, identified by Sage as an Arapaho, had found a glittering substance at the headwaters of the Kansas River and had made bullets of it.[26]

That Walking Whirlwind was still a prominent chief of the Cheyennes in 1844 is indicated by William Boggs, who mentioned him as fleeing with his band from a Delaware war party.[27] Boggs also stated that Chief Whirlwind was wounded in a battle with the Pawnees, a bullet striking him in the cheek.[28] Grinnell told of Old Whirlwind smoking the pipe for an expedition against the Pawnees in 1854.[29] Again in 1855, when all his horses had been stolen by the Pawnees, Walking Whirlwind borrowed a horse from the Kiowas and led an attack on a Pawnee camp on Cherry Brush Creek. The pony was very fast, and Walking Whirlwind was the first to count a coup against the Pawnees.[30]

Grinnell, who interviewed a Chief Whirlwind after 1900, also told a story of a fight with the Sac and Fox Indians on the Kansas River in 1854 and of how Whirlwind's reputation was greatly enhanced when nearly all of the feathers were shot from the war bonnet he was wearing.[31] There is little question that this was a different chief from the earlier Walking Whirlwind. When interviewed in 1879 by a government commission investigating the

Whirlwind, photographed by William S. Soule at Fort Sill, ca. 1870. *Courtesy of Smithsonian Institution, Bureau of American Ethnology Collection, Neg. No. 365-d.*

trek of the Northern Cheyennes from the Darlington Agency back to the north country in 1878, Southern Cheyenne Chief Whirlwind stated that he had been a chief for about fifteen years.[32] This would mean he had become a chief around 1864, possibly after a number of the older chiefs were killed at Sand Creek.

Likely this chief was the same Whirlwind who signed the Treaty of Medicine Lodge in 1867 and the Whirlwind who was against going to war in 1874 at Darlington and moved his band in near the agency.[33] General Nelson A. Miles reported that in July, 1874, Whirlwind told him that three Cheyenne braves and a woman had visited his camp and admitted to the killing of a white man between the Cimarron and Kingfisher station.[34] When free-lance reporter and western artist Frederic Remington visited the Darlington Agency in 1888, he cited Whirlwind as the head chief there.[35]

5

"Nothing Lives Long"

White Antelope

Ever since I went to Washington and received this
medal, I have called all white men as my brothers, but
other Indians have since been to Washington and got
medals, and now the soldiers do not shake hands, but
seek to kill me.

White Antelope

White Antelope[1] did a great deal to keep peace between the
Cheyennes and the white people; he would undoubtedly have
done much more had he not been killed by United States troops
at Sand Creek. He died, in fact, walking toward the soldiers of
Colonel John M. Chivington's command without a weapon, bullets flying about him, to tell the troops that the Cheyenne camp
was peaceful. Thus dying, when he could have been escaping to
save his own life, White Antelope was a martyr to the cause of
peace.

Like all Cheyenne chiefs, White Antelope had in his earlier
years been a great warrior. It has been said that he was with
Yellow Wolf when he raided the Kiowa horse herd on the North
Fork of the Red River in 1826, and he is credited with taking
part in the battle against the Kiowas and Comanches on Wolf
Creek.[2] Grinnell described White Antelope as a leading peacemaker between the Cheyennes and the Comanches and Kiowas
in 1840. Because he was among the bravest and strongest of
the Dog Soldiers, he was assigned along with Little Old Man
to go out and talk with the warrior band about making peace.
The Dog Soldiers put the matter in the hands of the two spokes-
men, and White Antelope and Little Old Man went back and told
the chiefs that the Dog Soldiers were willing to make peace.[3]

Most of this account, though recited through memory, is ver-
ified to some extent by White Antelope's prominence in the
tribe. An old frontiersman named Bill Hamilton claimed that

when he and a party of eight free trappers arrived at Cherry Creek in the spring of 1842, they found a Cheyenne village encamped there under Chief White Antelope. The traders were treated in a very friendly way and stayed with the Cheyennes for some time, trading and hunting. Again, in 1848, Hamilton was with a party near Ash Hollow when they were visited by about seventy-five Cheyennes led by White Antelope, "a noted chief and a proud and fine-looking warrior."[4]

William Boggs stated that White Antelope made a successful raid on the Pawnees by himself in the winter of 1844. He went on foot and was gone for five or six weeks. The tribe had given him up for dead when finally he returned with eleven Pawnee scalps.[5]

The first appearance of White Antelope in actual record was at the Treaty of Fort Laramie in 1851. Though he was not one of the principal chiefs to sign the treaty, he was chosen as one of the three men worthy of accompanying the commissioners to visit the Great Father in Washington, along with Alights-on-the-Cloud and Little Chief.[6] White Antelope was, however, a signer of the amended version of the treaty in 1853 on the South Platte River.

When he returned to the plains from Washington, White Antelope strove to keep peace with the whites, despite increasing friction on the Platte River. He was with the large body of Cheyennes that was attacked on the Republican River in late July, 1857, by General Edwin V. Sumner.[7] Following some disturbances on the Platte in 1856, the army had concluded that a punitive campaign against the Cheyennes was necessary. Sumner sent one column of troops, under Major John Sedgwick, up the Arkansas River past Bent's Fort and took another column up the Platte River himself. He rendezvoused his forces on the South Platte near the abandoned Fort St. Vrain. With a force of some four hundred troops and four mountain howitzers, Sumner headed eastward to the Solomon River of western Kansas, where his scouts had spotted Indian signs. On July 29 he left his wagon train behind and pushed ahead to engage a large force of Cheyenne warriors who had made medicine against the white men's bullets. Sumner, however, chose to make a saber attack, which unnerved the Cheyennes and put them to rout.

Three months later, in October, 1857, White Antelope and

three other chiefs appeared at Bent's Fort on the Arkansas River, insisting that the attack had been unwarranted. It had been the North Platte Cheyennes, the Dog Soldiers, who had committed the depredations against the whites on the North Platte River. "We are separate and distinct bands. . . . they have their own rules and regulations," the chiefs claimed.[8]

Events on the plains took a sudden and dramatic turn just a year later, when in November of 1858 the Russell group arrived at the mouth of Cherry Creek in search of gold. The resulting rush of gold-crazy whites across the plains was nothing less than a wholesale invasion of lands acknowledged to belong to the Cheyennes and Arapahoes by the Treaty of Fort Laramie.

Colonel W. A. Phillips visited the central plains in 1859, and his party came upon a great camp of the Cheyennes on the Upper Saline River. There they met White Antelope and other chiefs, to whom they gave presents. "White Antelope took what he got and divided it among his people, and then, folding his blanket across his breast retired to his tent. It was a romantic and inspiring scene."[9]

The necessity of redefining the relationship with the Indians and of establishing legal control over lands invaded by white citizens soon became apparent to the government. In the fall of 1860, Commissioner of Indian Affairs A. B. Greenwood came to Bent's New Fort on the Arkansas River to council with the Arapahoes and Cheyennes and get them to sign a new treaty. Even at the time, Fort Wise was being constructed just above the new fort Bent had built in 1853.

John Smith was sent out to bring in the Cheyenne and Arapaho chiefs, and during the middle of September he returned with White Antelope, Black Kettle, and several subchiefs. White Antelope and Black Kettle, along with Lean Bear, Little Wolf, Tall Bear, and Left Hand (an Arapaho who was living with the Cheyennes and signed with them), signed the Treaty of Fort Wise on February 18, 1861.[10]

A letter from Denver on September 30, 1860, reported that "White Antelope and Black Kettle expressed their willingness to enter into the arrangement but are such tenacious sticklers for squatter's sovereignty that they would not undertake to bind the tribes until the question should be submitted to a vote of all their braves. Finally decided matters should wait until papers sent out that fall or spring."[11] The agreements of this treaty were not far from what Yellow Wolf had recommended many years before. The Cheyennes agreed to settle on a small reserve in Colorado, with allotted lands for each family, and to learn to become farmers with the help of the government.

Only slight progress, however, was made by the government to implement the assistance promised the tribes. A small agency building was constructed upriver from Bent's Old Fort, and a patch of corn was planted. In the fall of 1861, Agent Albert G. Boone took a census of the Cheyennes on the Upper Arkansas River, which was necessary for the allotment of lands, and found there to be some 250 lodges with 425 men, 480 women, and 475 children for a total of 1,380 Cheyennes.[12]

With the outbreak of the Civil War in the spring of 1861, the efforts of the government to carry out the Fort Wise commitments were limited. Further, it soon became clear that the Cheyennes were not ready to settle down on the small, gameless reserve. Instead the bands hung to the buffalo lands of western Kansas and eastern Colorado, growing increasingly belligerent over the heavy flow of white immigration across their hunting grounds. They particularly objected to the traffic along the Smoky Hill River, where the whites had opened a new trail to the gold mines.

In August, 1863, the territorial governor of Colorado, John Evans, sent out trader Elbridge Gerry to meet with the Cheyennes. Gerry found the Indians on Beaver Creek in eastern Colorado. He called a council with several of the chiefs, including White Antelope, but the chiefs refused to attend. They said that a severe outbreak of whooping cough and diarrhea among them had recently killed thirty-five of their children. The war chiefs also said that the Treaty of Fort Wise was a swindle and claimed that both White Antelope and Black Kettle denied having signed the treaty. The buffalo would last a hundred years yet, they maintained, and they would not move to the Arkansas River where there was no game.[13]

The organization of military forces in Colorado Territory, brought on by the Civil War, also portended serious trouble for the Indians. Following the great victory of the Coloradoans over the Texas Confederate Army at La Glorieta Pass in New Mexico, the First Regiment of Colorado Volunteers returned to Colorado as a mounted home guard under Colonel John M.

Chivington. When charges of stock stealing were made against the Indians by Colorado settlers, Chivington and Governor Evans took a hard-line approach and ordered troops of the First out to kill any Indians they could catch. As a result, conflicts with Cheyennes occurred in Colorado during the spring and summer of 1864, with several small Cheyenne encampments captured and destroyed.

The most serious of these involved a Colorado force under Lieutenant George S. Eayre, who crossed the lines of his military district into Kansas and advanced on a force of Cheyennes who were holding their summer's buffalo hunt near the Smoky Hill River. When Cheyenne chiefs Lean Bear and Star rode forward to indicate their peaceful intent, they were shot down by Eayre's men. This incident touched off a bloody war of retaliation throughout Kansas by the Cheyennes during the summer of 1864.

In late August, 1864, the peace faction of the Cheyennes, led by White Antelope and Black Kettle, dispatched a letter to Fort Lyon (formerly Fort Wise), asking that peace be reestablished. Major Edward Wynkoop was influenced in his decision by the post interpreter, Cheyenne squawman John S. Smith, and he led an expedition into the heart of Indian country, meeting with the Cheyennes on the Smoky Hill River. After talking with Wynkoop, chiefs White Antelope, Black Kettle, and Bull Bear of the Cheyennes and four Arapahoes agreed to accompany the major to Denver for a council with Governor Evans and Colonel Chivington. It was an act of courage for the chiefs, for there were many among them who said it was dangerous and unwise to trust the word of a white man. White Antelope expressed this in a speech he made during the council held at Camp Weld in Denver on September 28, 1864:

When we sent our letter to Major Wynkoop, it was like going through a strong fire, or blast, for Major Wynkoop's men to come to our camp; it was the same for us to come to see you. We have our doubts whether the Indians south of the Arkansas, or those north of the Platte, will do as you say. A large number of Sioux have crossed the Platte in the vicinity of the Junction, into our country. When Major Wynkoop came, we proposed to make peace. He said he had no power to make peace, except to bring us here and return us safe.

63

White Antelope (*seated far left*), Black Kettle (*seated at center*), and Bull Bear (*seated on right of Black Kettle*) at the September, 1864, meeting at Denver. Other notables include John Simpson Smith (*standing third from left*) and Major Edward W. Wynkoop and Silas S. Soule (*squatting in front*). *Courtesy of State Historical Society of Colorado Library.*

White Antelope also told how he felt about the situation between the Cheyennes and the whites:

> I understand every word you have said, and will hold on to it. I will give you an answer directly. The Cheyennes, all of them, have their ears open this way, and they will hear what you say. I am proud to have seen the chief of all the whites in this country. I will tell my people. Ever since I went to Washington and received this medal, I have called all white men as my brothers, but other Indians have since been to Washington and got medals, and now the soldiers do not shake hands, but seek to kill me."[14]

White Antelope then promised Evans that he had "taken you

by the hand, and will tell the truth, keeping back nothing." He answered to the best of his ability all questions asked him relative to the troubles on the plains. The council was ended when Chivington, a former minister, took the floor and said: "I am not a big war chief, but all the soldiers in this country are at my command. My rule of fighting white men or Indians is, to fight them until they lay down their arms and submit to military authority. You are nearer Major Wynkoop than any one else, and you can go to him when you get ready to do that."

The chiefs appropriately considered Chivington's words to be a promise of protection if they would take their families in to Fort Lyon. Upon returning to the plains, White Antelope and Black Kettle began moving their village toward Fort Lyon, encamping at the bend of Sand Creek, about forty miles above the post. During a preliminary visit to Lyon, the chiefs found that Major Wynkoop, whose Indian policy had been too liberal for the army, had been replaced by Major Scott Anthony. Anthony told the Indians that he was unable to feed them and that they should remain at the bend of Sand Creek, where they would not be bothered by government troops and where they could better hunt for their own subsistence.

Meanwhile, Colonel Chivington, caught up in the ambition of territorial politics and military prestige and fearful that one-hundred-day time limit of the recently formed Colorado Third Volunteer Regiment would expire without his proving its necessity for enlistment, had decided on a campaign against the Indians. With a snowstorm and bitter cold gripping Colorado, he moved units of the Colorado First and Colorado Third to the Arkansas River and marched downriver toward Lyon.

Major Anthony was quick to go along with Chivington's plan to attack the Sand Creek village, despite the opposition of such officers as Captain Silas Soule and others who agreed with the peacemaking policies of Wynkoop. Making an all-night forced march, Chivington and his army of some seven hundred mounted troops approached the Sand Creek village at daybreak on the morning of November 29, 1864. They found the Cheyenne camp nestled in a bend where the small creek looped around a range of low sand hills.

The village, which was clustered along the flat bank on the north side, contained the lodges of most of the peace chiefs of the Southern Cheyennes: White Antelope; Black Kettle; War Bonnet and Standing-in-Water, who had been to Washington in 1863 to visit President Abraham Lincoln; the renowned Yellow Wolf; subchief One Eye, who had carried the peace letter to Fort Lyon; and Arapaho Chief Left Hand. All of these, with the sole exception of Black Kettle, would be killed on this day of Chivington's infamy.

A squaw out gathering wood alerted the village only moments before the troops struck the camp. White Antelope joined Black Kettle in front of his lodge, and together they used a lodge pole to raise a large American flag that Commissioner A. B. Greenwood had given Black Kettle in 1860. They called out to the village to be calm, explaining that they were under the protection of the troops.[15] Then the soldiers began to fire with their pistols, rifles, and even the cannon they had with them. The people began running in all directions as the columns of yelling, blue-coated troops bore down on them from all sides. The narrow, dry-bedded channel of Sand Creek offered the only avenue of escape, but many were caught there and shot down by the soldiers.

White Antelope, desperately trying to prove his friendship for the whites, ran forward with his hand high in the air, shouting "Stop! Stop!" in clear English.[16] He advanced to within fifteen or twenty steps of the line of troops, but the soldiers paid no attention to him. Bullets were cutting the air all around him. Finally, he saw it was hopeless to try to stop the soldiers. He stood in the center of Sand Creek, folded his arms over his chest, and began his death song: "Nothing lives long, except the earth and the mountains."[17] The soldiers shot him down. Later, while the soldiers were celebrating their victory with whisky, they scalped White Antelope, then cut off his nose, ears, and even his scrotum to be used for a tobacco pouch.[18]

6

Friend of the White Father

Lean Bear

*He said the President's invitation for them to come
hither had traveled a long way over mountains, rivers
and plains, until reaching the villages, where it had
been gratefully accepted. . . . He was ready to hear
what the President had to say; had no pockets in
which to hide his words, but would treasure them in
his heart, and would faithfully carry them back to his
people.*

Words of Lean Bear as reported by *Washington Evening Star*

In May, 1864, Cheyenne Chief Lean Bear[1] rode forward from
where his people were holding a buffalo hunt on the Smoky Hill
River to meet a column of United States troops that had suddenly appeared from the west. On his chest Lean Bear wore a
peace medal, and in his hand he carried a paper verifying that he
was peaceful and a friend of the whites. But the troops commenced firing, knocking him from his horse. Then the soldiers
shot him several more times as he lay on the ground. The piece
of paper fluttered away in the prairie wind. All the troops were
firing, and no one bothered to get the paper. No one knew that
it had been signed personally by the president of the United
States of America, Abraham Lincoln, but likely none would have
cared. The troops, under Lieutenant George S. Eayre, were intent on following the orders of Colonel John M. Chivington in
Colorado to kill Indians whenever and wherever found on the
plains. Lean Bear was an Indian, and it mattered not that he had
been personally vouched for by President Lincoln.

Lean Bear's name first appears in the historical records in
connection with an incident on the Santa Fe Trail in 1851. In
June of that year Agent Thomas Fitzpatrick sent out runners to
call the plains tribes together for a council at Fort Atkinson, near

the present site of Dodge City, Kansas. His purpose was to persuade them to attend the big peace council at Fort Laramie in the north. Within a couple of weeks the country on either side of the Arkansas River was virtually covered with Comanche, Kiowa, Apache, Arapaho, and Cheyenne lodges. Fitzpatrick provided a small feast of bread, pork, and coffee and gave each band some small presents. He conducted talks with each tribe. The Cheyennes and Arapahoes agreed to attend, but the Comanches, Kiowas, and Apaches refused to take their horse herds north among such noted horse stealers as the Crows and the Sioux.[2]

After the council ended, the tribes were preparing to leave, when Colonel E. V. Sumner arrived at Fort Atkinson with a military command en route to New Mexico. Sumner encamped near a very large Cheyenne village and proceeded to recruit horses and mules from the tribe. During the two days of trading, the Indians were allowed free access to the military camp as well as to Fort Atkinson. Fitzpatrick feared that such free intercourse between the Indians and the whites was bound to lead to trouble, and it did.

A youthful Cheyenne warrior named Lean Bear saw a glittering ring on the hand of an officer's wife who was with Sumner's command. With his fascination for trinkets, beads, and jewelry, Lean Bear took hold of the woman's hand to get a closer look. The woman was both alarmed and insulted, and she cried out. Her husband came rushing up, struck Lean Bear with his carriage whip, and, according to Fitzpatrick, gave the Cheyenne warrior "a good sound flogging."

To strike a brave with a whip was a grave insult among the Cheyennes, who would not hit a male child even for disciplinary purposes lest it break his spirit as a warrior. Lean Bear painted his face black and white, mounted his war-horse, and rode about the Cheyenne camp with a big tomahawk in his hand, haranguing his fellow warriors to attack the whites.[3] The entire Cheyenne camp became "very much exasperated" and demanded that Fitzpatrick provide some sort of reparation that, according to Cheyenne custom, would compensate for the insult done to them. Fitzpatrick refused, and a short time later a group of Kiowas and Comanches came to Fitzpatrick and said that the Cheyennes were planning to attack the agent's camp.

Sumner, in the meantime, had struck his tents and resumed his march for New Mexico. Fitzpatrick quickly dispatched word to him of the impending attack, whereupon Sumner counter-marched his dragoons and planted them a short distance from the Cheyenne camp. The move greatly alarmed the Cheyennes, and a delegation of chiefs visited Fitzpatrick to deny the report the Kiowas and Comanches had given him. A blanket was presented to Lean Bear as an "unction to his wounds," and the matter was settled.

It is not surprising that in his younger days Lean Bear was a hot-blooded warrior. But all that is known about him as a chief clearly demonstrates that he was a peacemaker in the true tradition of a Cheyenne chief. On October 28, 1857, William Bent wrote a letter from his fort on the Arkansas River, indicating that he had been visited by four Cheyenne chiefs who were concerned about Sumner's attack on them two months earlier on the Republican River. One of these chiefs was "Starved Bear," or Lean Bear. They wanted the government to send someone out to talk with them.[4] The government responded in 1860, when Commissioner A. B. Greenwood met with them at Fort Wise, and Lean Bear was one of the principal signers of the treaty in 1861.[5]

With the outbreak of the Civil War, the government became concerned that the wild tribes of the plains would lend support to the Confederate cause. In fact, some overtures were made by the rebels in this direction, particularly with the tribes in Indian Territory, now Oklahoma. To counteract this threat, and to soothe relations with the frontier tribes, arrangements were made in the spring of 1863 for a delegation of chiefs to visit Washington. Through the efforts of John Smith, several chiefs then in the vicinity of Fort Larned were persuaded to make the trip: Lean Bear, War Bonnet, and Standing-in-Water, of the Cheyennes; Spotted Wolf and Neva, of the Arapahoes; Lone Wolf, Yellow Wolf, White Bull, Yellow Buffalo, and Little Heart, of the Kiowas; Ten Bears and Pricked Forehead, of the Comanches; Poor Bear, of the Apaches; and Jacob, of the Caddos. Two Kiowa women, Coy and Etla, went along.[6]

Accompanied by Smith and Agent Samuel G. Colley, the chiefs arrived at Leavenworth on March 12, where they were lodged at the Planters Hotel. From Leavenworth the delegation traveled by stagecoach to Saint Louis and from there by train to Washington, D.C. On the morning of March 26, 1863, Lean Bear and the other chiefs were taken to the White House for an interview with the "White Chief," Abraham Lincoln. The *Washington Evening Star* described the event as follows:

> The delegation of wild Indians of the Plains now on a visit to Washington, accompanied by their interpreters and agents, called upon the President at the Executive Mansion this forenoon. A rumor of their intended call brought together a large assemblage of gentlemen and ladies, including a number of foreign ministers and their families, the Secretary of the Interior, Commissioner of Indian Affairs, Assistant Secretary of the Navy, the Hon. D. S. Dickinson, Lord Lyons, Secretaries Chase and Seward, M. Lisbon's family, ex-Gov. Bashford, Amos Reed, Esq., Secretary to the Superintendent of Indian Affairs in Utah, and others of note.
>
> The savages were dressed in full feather—buffalo robes, Indian tanned, and bead worked leggings, with a profusion of paints upon their faces and hair, &c., &c. On entering the East Room they squatted themselves down upon the floor in a semicircle— fourteen chiefs and two squaws—and were instantly surrounded by the curious crowd, quite as gaudily if not quite so fantastically caparisoned.[7]

After a fifteen-minute wait, President Lincoln entered the room. Following a brief introduction by Superintendent of Indian Affairs William P. Dole, John Smith introduced each chief by name to the president. The chiefs rose in succession and shook the president's hand "with expressement" and then immediately resumed their seats on the floor.[8] The *Washington Evening Star* continued:

> The President remarked to the interpreter that he was too glad to see them here, and was ready to hear anything they had to say. On this being interpreted to the Indians, Lean Bear answered (in his vernacular) that he had much to say to him, but was so nervous that he desired a chair on which to sit when making his talk. One was at once procured, and he proceeded to deliver himself of quite a lengthy speech, which was interpreted (in paragraphs) by an intelligent interpreter at his side. He expressed his thanks to the interpreter, the agent, and all other whites who had facilitated them upon their long journey. He said the President's invitation for them to come hither had traveled a long way over mountains, rivers, and plains, until reaching the villages, where it had been

Delegation of chiefs, including Lean Bear, with White House onlookers in Washington, D.C., 1863. *Far left,* John Simpson Smith and Agent Samuel G. Colley; *far right,* Mrs. Abraham Lincoln. Lean Bear is probably one of the two Indians seated on the far left. *Courtesy of Lloyd Ostendorf.*

gratefully accepted. They were of different tribes, but were really one people or race, with common interests and customs. He was ready to hear what the President had to say; had no pockets in which to hide his words, but would treasure them in his heart, and would faithfully carry them back to his people. The President he said lived in splendor, with a far better and finer wigwam than he

71

had at home, yet he too was like the President, a great chief at home.

He asked the President to counsel his white children on the Plains, so that there would be no more war between them and the whites, his purpose being to make traveling over the plains as safe to the whites as possible. He wished to live in peace for the balance of his life, on the buffalo, as his fathers had done, while they lasted, and again urged the President to counsel his white children, who were annually encroaching more and more upon their tribes, to abstain from acts of violence and wrong towards them. He deplored, he said, the war between the whites, now being waged, and expressed the determination of the tribes not to take part or sides in it, and said that its end would be hailed with joy by them. As they were all leading chiefs of their respective tribes, their return home was necessary, and he asked the President to expedite it, so that they might get there as soon as possible.[9]

Some of the other chiefs also made speeches, echoing Lean Bear's hope for peace on the plains. President Lincoln then addressed the chiefs. He told them that the white people considered the world to be a great ball, and he had a Professor Henry show them a globe and the relative locations of Washington, D.C., and their own country. Lincoln said:

We have people now present from all parts of the globe—here, and here, and here. There is a great difference between this palefaced people and their red brethren, both as to numbers and the way in which they live. We know not whether your own situation is best for your race, but this is what has made the difference in our way of living.

The palefaced people are numerous and prosperous because they cultivate the earth, produce bread, and depend upon the products of the earth rather than wild game for a subsistence.

This is the chief reason of the difference; but there is another. Although we are now engaged in a great war between one another, we are not, as a race, so much disposed to fight and kill one another as our red brethren.

You have asked for my advice. I really am not capable of advising you whether, in the providence of the Great Spirit, who is the great Father of us all, it is for you to maintain the habits and customs of your race, or adopt a new mode of life.

I can only say that I can see no way in which your race is to become as numerous and prosperous as the white race except by living as they do, by the cultivation of the earth.

72

It is the object of this Government to be on terms of peace with you and with all our red brethren. We constantly endeavor to be so. We make treaties with you, and will try to observe them; and if our children should sometimes behave badly, and violate these treaties, it is against our wish.

You know it is not always possible for any father to have his children do precisely as he wishes them to do.

In regard to being sent back to your own country, we have an officer, the Commissioner of Indian Affairs, who will take charge of that matter, and make the necessary arrangements.[10]

With that the president arose and, commencing with Lean Bear, shook hands with all the chiefs. Through Smith, Lean Bear thanked the president for his kindness. Afterward the members of the delegation were escorted to the conservatory of the White House, where a Brady photographer took their pictures with various persons standing behind, one of them being Mrs. Lincoln.[11]

President Lincoln had passed over to Commissioner Dole the Indians' request for a speedy return home. But it was not to be. The delegation remained in Washington for several days, touring the city, visiting government facilities, and even attending a play at Grover's Theatre. Finally, as they were about to depart for the plains, a letter arrived from New York City for Agent Colley. It was from the famous P. T. Barnum, who had read of the chiefs' visit to Washington. Always searching for new attractions for his museum, Barnum invited the chiefs to visit New York City. "I can show them a million curiosities from all parts of the earth," Barnum promised, "and taking them to the top of the building, can present them a *coup d'oeil* of New York in its glory, wealth and maritime greatness, which will ineffaceably endure on their memories to the latest hour of their lives."[12]

He also promised that he would give the chiefs valuable presents during their visit and would spare neither money nor pains to make the chiefs, as well as the agent and interpreter, comfortable. The invitation was too good for Colley to turn down. He accepted, forewarning Barnum that the "Indians have never slept on beds and must have rooms where they can spread out blankets on the floor." It would be necessary to "procure bread, raw beef, and coffee, all of which they will cook in their own rude Indian style." The Indians would also need some paint and oil.[13]

Lean Bear and the other chiefs arrived in New York City on

Three of the delegation of chiefs in Washington, D.C., 1863. Agent Samuel G. Colley is on the left. Lean Bear is possibly second from the right. *Courtesy of the British Museum.*

April 8, coincidental to a Barnum advertisement that appeared in the *New York Times* on the same day:

TODAY

AN EXTRAORDINARY SIGHT IN NEW YORK
First Appearance of the
GREAT INDIAN CHIEFS AND WARRIORS
who have just arrived from Washington where they
have been on a visit to their "Great Father," the
PRESIDENT OF THE UNITED STATES
all of them being fully attired in their
WAR-PAINT, WAMPUM AND FEATHERS
and presenting the most attractive features of the
REDMAN IN HIS NATIVE GRANDEUR
fresh from the hunting grounds and
WIGWAMS OF HIS WILD ABODES[14]

The newspapers of New York reacted with amused derision of the untutored savages of the plains who fought over trinkets thrown to them. The *Times* observed: "The Wild Indians still remain under the cheerful impression that they are the guests of the City, that Barnum is the Great Mogul, and the Museum is his palace."[15] On April 11 the newspaper reported:

> The Indian chiefs and squaws which are now exhibiting at the Museum, visited yesterday morning Public School No. 14, on Twenty-seventh street, near Third Avenue. They were accompanied by Mr. Barnum and by Mr. Smith, who acts as interpreter. They were conveyed to the school in an omnibus drawn by six horses, which was preceded by a vehicle containing a band of musicians. Their appearance on Broadway and other streets through which they passed excited great attention, and by the time the building was reached, a large concourse of people began to assemble in the vicinity.
>
> The Indians appeared highly pleased at the calisthenic exercise performed by the children, and listened attentively to some delightful singing, although, of course, the words were unintelligible to them. "War Bonnet," upon being invited to speak, declined, for the reason that everything was new to him, and he could say nothing which would be satisfactory to those present. Before taking leave they stood in line, while Mr. Smith designated each one by his and her name, and the tribe to which they belonged, and also intimated their dispositions, giving "Yellow Buffalo" the credit of being the best Indian, and "Little Heart" the discredit of being the worse one.... the unique party remained about an hour, and were then conducted to the omnibus and driven down Broadway.[16]

On April 18 the chiefs made their last appearance on Barnum's stage, Smith helping Lean Bear and the others make farewell speeches to the New Yorkers. Finally, in early May the chiefs were back once more in their own world, perhaps wondering if the whole thing had not been just a wild dream.

Despite the words of friendship spoken by President Lincoln, Lean Bear found that troubles between the whites and the Indians were increasing on the central plains. A large camp of Cheyennes under Lean Bear and Black Kettle spent the winter of 1863–64 on Ash Creek near Fort Larned. During the spring of 1864, news of the attacks upon Cheyennes along the South Platte River and in eastern Colorado caused considerable nervousness among the people. At mid-May they broke camp and began moving northward to join other Cheyenne bands, hunting on the way. After a march of one day they went into camp on the Smoky Hill River. One morning some buffalo hunters who had gone out early returned to camp to report that they had seen a column of soldiers with cannon approaching from the west.

Lean Bear mounted his horse and with a large escort rode out to meet the soldiers. When the Indians appeared, the troops were ordered into battle formation. Lean Bear told his warriors to stay where they were, and, accompanied by another Cheyenne named Star, he road forward with his peace medal on his chest and carrying the paper given him by President Lincoln. But when he was some twenty or thirty yards away, the officer in charge of the troops ordered the men to fire. Lean Bear and Star both fell to the ground in front of the troops, who continued to shoot them.[17] As Lincoln had said, it is not always possible for a father to get his children to do as he wishes.

Southern Cheyenne chiefs Cloud Chief, Little Bear, and Little Chief at Concho Indian School, Indian Territory. *Courtesy of El Reno Carnegie Library.*

Lesser Cheyenne chiefs at Darlington Agency, circa 1890. *Courtesy of Western History Collections, University of Oklahoma Library.*

Southern Cheyennes Henry Roman Nose, Yellow Bear, and Lame Man (also known as Cohoe) after their release from Fort Marion, Florida. This Roman Nose should not be confused with the warrior who was killed at Beecher's Island. *Courtesy of Smithsonian Institution, National Anthropological Archives, Neg. No. 345.*

Chief Henry Roman Nose and wife at Watonga, Oklahoma. *Courtesy of Central State University Museum, Edmond, Oklahoma.*

Chief Wolf Robe. *Courtesy of Western History Collections, University of Oklahoma Library.*

Above: Chief Wolf Robe at sixty-eight in 1909. Photograph by DeLancey Gill. *Courtesy of American Ethnology Collection, Neg. No. 303-B.*

Facing page, top: Chief Magpie, 1924. Photograph by DeLancey Gill. *Courtesy of Smithsonian Institution, National Anthropological Archives, Neg. No. 230.*

Facing page, bottom: Chief Turkey Leg, a noted Northern Cheyenne chief. This photograph was taken at Watonga, Oklahoma, circa 1900. *Courtesy of the Central State University Museum, Edmond, Oklahoma.*

Turkey Leg
Cheif N. Cheyenne
© P. Chaufty Studio

Bull Bear, leader of the Cheyenne Dog Soldiers for many years. As early as 1864 Bull Bear offered to fight on the side of the whites but was refused by John Chivington. *Courtesy of Smithsonian Institution, National Anthropological Archives, Neg. No. T-11,853.*

7

The Warrior Leaders

Bull Bear, Tall Bull, Roman Nose

I have given my word to fight with the whites. My brother, Lean Bear, died in trying to keep peace with the whites. I am willing to die in the same way, and expect to do so.

Bull Bear

The Dog Soldiers were originally a warrior society, but when Porcupine Bear committed his disgrace in 1838, he and his followers and family were outlawed, and they eventually formed a separate division of the tribe.[1] Following the trouble on the Platte River in 1856 and Sumner's ensuing attack on the tribe, the Dog Soldiers and the Arkansas River bands were at odds. The Dogs ranged along the Smoky Hill and Republican rivers, appointing their own leading men and refusing to have anything to do with the Southern Cheyenne bands who would not join them in their wars.

Thus the Cheyennes, who had split into two divisions during the early part of the century, had now become essentially three units: the Northern Cheyennes north of the Platte River, the Dog Soldiers or Central Cheyennes, and the Southern Cheyennes along the Arkansas River.[2] Numbering around a hundred lodges, a strong band, the Dog Soldiers often threatened to go north of the Platte River and take back their old lands, but they never tried. They were generally mean to white traders, sometimes throwing their trade goods in the fire. This warlike central group was a magnet to young hostiles from the south who were ready to make war against the whites. After the Sand Creek Massacre the Dog Soldiers were joined by most of the young warriors, including mixed bloods such as George and Charlie Bent and Edmond Guerrier. It was mostly the older peace chiefs and their families who remained in the south with Black Kettle.

The leader of the Dog Soldiers in 1864 was Bull Bear,[3]

brother of the murdered Lean Bear. Despite his brother's murder, Bull Bear was willing to accompany Edward W. Wynkoop and the other chiefs to Denver to talk with Governor John Evans. During the Camp Weld conference, Evans asked the Indians what the Sioux were going to do next. Bull Bear, a big, strong man, answered: "Their intention is to clear out all this country. They are angry, and will do all the damage to the whites they can. I am with you and the troops to fight all those who have no ears to listen to what you say. Who are they? Show them to me—I am young. I have never harmed a white man. I am pushing for something good. I am always going to be friendly with the whites; they can do me good."[4]

Later he repeated his offer: "I have given my word to fight with the whites. My brother, Lean Bear, died in trying to keep peace with the whites. I am willing to die in the same way, and expect to do so."[5]

But rather than enlist Bull Bear's help, Evans and Chivington chose instead to attack Black Kettle's peaceful band at Sand Creek, sting the fury of the Dog Soldiers, and ignite again the war on the plains. Instead of accepting a powerful ally, they made a powerful enemy. Never again would the Cheyenne Dog Soldier trust the whites, and in the years following the Civil War they would offer a troublesome barrier to the expansion of settlements and railroads across the central plains.

In the months following Sand Creek, Bull Bear's Dog Soldiers made "war to the knife" against the whites in Kansas, Colorado, and Nebraska. Bolstered by most of the young braves from the Central and Southern bands as well as by the Arapahoes and the Sioux, the Dog Soldiers struck at wagon routes and outlying settlements. Julesburg on the South Platte trail was burned, and Lieutenant Colonel William O. Collins, riding in relief of the post, was driven back to Fort Laramie. Other attempts to quell the Indians with the inadequate frontier military force available in 1865 failed.

Meanwhile, the Sand Creek controversy had spawned congressional and army investigations, and President Andrew Johnson authorized a new treaty to be made with the Cheyennes and Arapahoes, Kiowas and Comanches, and Plains Apaches. But the treaty council that met in August, 1865, at the mouth of the Little Arkansas River produced only the Cheyenne peace chiefs—Black Kettle, Little Robe, and five other chiefs. Bull Bear and the Dog Soldiers refused to attend the council, unwilling to forgive the whites for Sand Creek, though there is evidence that Dog Soldier leader Tall Bull did put his mark to an amended version of the treaty later.[6]

The Indian war in western Kansas continued into 1866, with the Dog Soldiers declaring their determination not to give up their hunting grounds on the Smoky Hill and Republican rivers. They were further incensed by the opening of the stage route from Leavenworth to Denver along the Smoky Hill, and in October, 1866, forty Dog Soldiers led by Bull Bear attacked the stage station at Chalk Bluffs and killed two station keepers.[7] Other similar depredations were reported.

In the fall of 1866 the newly organized Seventh Cavalry went into training at Fort Riley, Kansas, and Major General Winfield Scott Hancock arrived to take command of the military Department of the Missouri. A Civil War hero now with presidential ambition, Hancock organized an expedition against the Indians of western Kansas, principally the Cheyennes. In the spring of 1867, Hancock and Lieutenant Colonel George Armstrong Custer, commanding the Seventh Cavalry, marched to Fort Larned at the mouth of the Pawnee Fork. Hancock sent out runners to call the Cheyenne chiefs in for a council, and some two hundred lodges of Cheyennes and Sioux under Bull Bear and Pawnee Killer were located on the Pawnee Fork some forty miles above Larned. Despite a late spring snowstorm, Bull Bear, Tall Bull, White Horse, Little Robe, and other tribal leaders came to Hancock's tent and counciled with him around a huge fire.

Reporter Henry M. Stanley, destined for fame as the discoverer of Dr. David Livingstone in Africa, was there and described Bull Bear and the other chiefs:

> The Indians were dressed in various styles, many of them with the orthodox army overcoats, some with gorgeous red blankets, while their faces were painted and their bodies bedizened in all the glory of the Indian toilette. To the hideous slits in their ears were hanging large rings of brass; they wore armlets of silver, wrist rings of copper, necklaces of beads of variegated colours, breast ornaments of silver shields, and Johnson silver medals, and their scalplocks were adorned with a long string of thin silver discs.[8]

Hancock made a threatening speech to the chiefs, saying that he had heard that some Indians were trying to stir up a war to hurt the whites. If war came, he said, he had chiefs with him who had commanded many more men than the Indian chiefs had ever seen and who had fought more great battles than the Indian chiefs had fought fights. "If there are any good Indians, who don't want to go to war, I shall help them," Hancock said. "If there are any bad chiefs, I will help the good chiefs to put their heels on them." He explained that his generals would not derive any distinction from fighting such a small enemy and were not anxious for a conflict. But they knew how to fight and were ready for a "just war."

Hancock also insisted that the next day he was going to visit the Indians' villages. It was this point that most concerned Tall Bull when he answered the general: "The buffalo are diminishing fast. The antelope that were plenty a few years ago, they are now thin. When they will all die away we shall be hungry. We shall want something to eat, and we will be compelled to come into the fort. Your young men must not fire on us. Whenever they see us they fire, and we fire on them." Tall Bull paused here, then spoke his concern about Hancock and his troops coming to the Indian camps, remembering all too well the Sand Creek ordeal: "You say you are going to the village tomorrow. If you go, I shall have no more to say to you than here. I have said all I want to say here." Hancock interrupted, "Nonetheless, I am going to your camp tomorrow." Tall Bull said he could not speak for the Sioux who were at the encampment, and the meeting was closed.

Before noon the next day, when Hancock began his movement upriver toward the village, he and his army were met by some three hundred Cheyenne and Sioux warriors, all painted for war, their horses tails tied up and weapons ready. It was a tense moment and conflict seemed certain. But Major Edward W. Wynkoop, now agent for the Cheyennes and Arapahoes, rode forward and parleyed with Tall Bull and Bull Bear. Though still very suspicious and angry, the Indians withdrew. That night while the chiefs held another talk with Hancock, the villagers fled, leaving their lodges standing.

Hancock dispatched Custer and the Seventh Cavalry in pursuit, but the Civil War hero, inexperienced on the plains, completely lost the Indians when their trail repeatedly divided and divided until finally there was no trail left to follow. Hancock eventually burned the Indian village, with its 250 valuable skin lodges, robes, foodstuffs, and other worldly goods of the Indians, giving the Cheyenne warriors even further cause to distrust and hate the whites.

Hostilities continued during the summer and fall of 1867, with Custer and the Seventh Cavalry making empty sweeps of the Cheyenne hunting grounds on the Republican River of western Kansas and Nebraska. Now the Kansas-Pacific Railway was reaching out onto the prairies beyond Fort Hays, and Bull Bear's warriors, assisted by the Sioux under Pawnee Killer, virtually closed down the Smoky Hill trail to white commerce and travel.

With most of the fighting men of the Central and Southern Cheyennes under him, Bull Bear had now become one of the most powerful chiefs in the Cheyenne Nation. When the treaty council at Medicine Lodge Creek of southern Kansas was called in October, 1867, reporter Stanley was on hand again to write: "The Cheyenne tribe was represented by Black Kettle, formerly great sachem of the tribe, but who has lately been disposed because of his peaceful proclivities, and Bull Bear, a most powerful warrior, is substituted instead."[9] A reporter for the *Cincinnati Gazette* echoed the same opinion: "Bull Bear, Chief of Dog Soldiers of the Cheyennes, was in camp this morning, and says he will bring in the representative men of his bands. He is *the* man of the Cheyennes, and whatever steps he and his bands take, the Cheyenne nation will accept."[10]

Bull Bear met with the peace commissioners in a preliminary council and agreed to go out and bring in his Dog Soldier chiefs. He promised to have them at the treaty council in eight days if the commissioners would hold up the council until he returned, saying he wanted to hear what the other tribes, particularly the Kiowas, had to say about the Cheyennes.[11] Major General William S. Harney, a member of the commission, favored Bull Bear's suggestion:

> General Harney says that the Cheyennes are the most reliable of any of the hostile Indians, that they never break their word, that he has known them for forty-two years, and has always found them reliable. He thinks that Bull Bear is the ablest man of the Cheyenne nation, and the originator of all the Cheyenne attacks

during the season. Certain it is, that he has more influence over the young men of the nation than any other chief, and there are rumors that he is deposing Black Kettle, who has been friendly disposed to the whites.[12]

Though Bull Bear and the other Cheyenne chiefs visited the commission camp on occasion during the wait, it was not eight days but fourteen before the Cheyennes completed their Medicine Arrow renewal rites and came in, led by the Cheyenne Dog Soldiers:

> Toward noon a cloud of dust was seen rising southeast of the camp, and messengers came to bring the news of the approach of the Cheyennes. Are they peaceful or friendly was the first question, and as neither the interpreters nor commissioners could give satisfactory answers, it was deemed best to have the soldiers prepared with loaded guns, and the officers at their posts, ready on the least demonstration of hostility. Nearer came the dust cloud, and soon their yells, loud and defiant, rent the air. The friendly Indians, the Arrapahoes and Comanches, four hundred of whom were in camp, exhibited every sign of fear. They mounted their nags and rushed like mad out of camp. The Arrapahoes took the high hill at our rear on the right, and the Comanches the bluff on the left. They evidently deemed the Cheyennes to be hostile, but General Harney was confident they were friendly and insisted upon it "that he never knew a Cheyenne to break his word." Soon emerging from the woods on the other side of the river, the wild men of the plains—the bravest, ugliest, most vindictive and determined Indians of our day, the bone and marrow of Indian pluck; they who boast it is they that are never taken prisoners; they, whose squaws, at the Sand Creek massacre of 1864, stabbed themselves rather than fall into Chivington's hands; they, these hostile Cheyennes, four hundred strong, formed in a long line, reaching far below our camp, and now stood before us, within stone's throw. It was a grand sight—one we never expect again to witness.[13]

After a brief council on the following day, the weary and impatient commission persuaded the Cheyenne chiefs to sign the Medicine Lodge treaty papers. But the Indians signed only after Senator Henderson took some of the chiefs aside and promised them, contrary to the terms of the document, that they would still be able to roam and hunt the buffalo prairies of western Kansas. Even so Bull Bear was reluctant to sign:

Bull Bear, as he appeared in later life. After the Cheyennes were driven
to the reservation, Bull Bear was the first to send his son to a white
school. *Courtesy of Smithsonian Institution.*

It took half an hour to convince Bull Bear that he was in duty bound to sign. At last Gen. Harney got up, and brought up an argument in this wise: "The Great Father knows you are a chief, and your name must be seen upon its face, or he will not recognize it." This was a socdolger; he signed it at once, instead of touching the pen lightly, he pressed on the head of the pen until it was buried in the paper. He then turned to all, with a grim smile, and said, "I have done it, and my word shall last. One chief is enough to sign for us, but here are a dozen names."[14]

After the signing Senator Henderson invited Bull Bear to visit Washington. The Cheyenne chief considered the invitation and agreed that he might accept after the commission had concluded a treaty with the Northern bands of the tribe.[15]

TALL BULL

Another Cheyenne Dog Soldier chief who played a major role in the Medicine Lodge council was Tall Bull.[16] When the chiefs talked with Hancock on the Pawnee Fork, it was Tall Bull who answered Hancock's belligerent talk. He said that the Cheyennes did not want war and would not bother troops along the Smoky Hill River, that his tribe was at peace and had never done the whites harm. "Our agent told us to meet you here," Tall Bull told Hancock. "Whenever you want to go to the Smoky Hill you can do so. We are willing to be friends with the whites."[17]

Tall Bull was greatly alarmed at Hancock's threat to march his troops to the Cheyenne-Sioux village and urged Agent Wynkoop to try to change the officer's mind. Tall Bull later spoke of how he felt about Hancock's action. He said that when he had signed the Treaty of the Little Arkansas, he had intended to live by it, but "when we were treated so by General Hancock, I became ashamed that I had consented to the treaty; I was blind with rage, and what I have done since I am not ashamed of. I consented to give the whites the roads, any and all the roads they wanted, and I intended to let them have them, but I was with General Hancock just before he marched to our village, and told him not to go. He would go, and the war followed, and I have fought, and am not ashamed."[18]

When the peace commission first reached Medicine Lodge Creek in the fall of 1867, Tall Bull was one of the Cheyenne leaders to first visit the commission camp. He and Gray Head were recognized by Harney as chiefs he had known in 1858 on the northern plains, and the general invited the two Cheyenne chiefs into his tent.[19] On invitation, Tall Bull returned the next evening, leading about fifty Dog Soldiers mounted on splendid mules and singing their warrior songs.[20] It was reported that later Tall Bull and Gray Head had gone to Black Kettle's camp, which was pitched nearby, and Tall Bull had threatened Black Kettle. He said that if Black Kettle did not join the other Cheyennes in their Medicine Arrow ceremonies on the Cimarron River and explain what he hoped to gain from making peace with the whites, the Dog Soldiers would come in and kill all of his horses.[21]

Tall Bull and the other chiefs at the Medicine Lodge council were described by a reporter as "singularly fine looking men—splendidly framed, and with impressive, characteristic faces. They showed by every look and gesture their fitness for command. The more I see of these Cheyenne the higher opinion I have of them. They are better looking than the others; they are cleaner and more of the Spartan fire burns in their veins. Sooner death than captivity is the motto of these warriors of the plains."[22]

Neither Tall Bull nor Bull Bear was responsible for breaking the peace made at Medicine Lodge. During the spring of 1868, Tall Bull was one leader of a large force of Cheyenne warriors that advanced on the Kaw Agency at Council Grove, Kansas, to seek revenge against that tribe.[23] Only a minor skirmish resulted, though the Kansas populace was severely frightened by the band of armed Cheyennes riding through their settlements.

In August, two white scouts visited the Cheyenne camps above Fort Hays. Will Comstock and Sharp Grover were checking on the Indians for General Phil Sheridan. Bull Bear, though he knew the two men to be spies on his camp, followed Cheyenne custom and took them into his lodge, where they were given protection, shelter, and food. The next day as they were being escorted out of the camp, however, the two men were fired on by some of the young bucks, and Comstock was killed and Grover severely wounded.[24]

The two scouts had not realized the precariousness of their situation in the camp. Only a few days before their arrival at the Cheyenne camp, a war party of young men, including a few Arapahoes and Sioux, had gone off to raid the Pawnees. But instead, they had become involved in a series of brutal attacks on white settlements along the Saline and Solomon rivers of eastern Kansas. These acts broke the already shaky peace on the plains, re-ignited the war, and provided General Sheridan with the public support for a series of operations against the Cheyennes.

One of Sheridan's aggressions was the September intrusion of a fifty-man scouting force under Major George A. Forsyth into the Cheyenne-Sioux country of the Upper Republican River. It resulted in the classic battle of Beecher's Island in which the famous warrior Roman Nose was killed. The Dog Soldiers, under Bull Bear, Tall Bull, and White Horse, were involved in the affair. The combined Cheyenne-Arapaho-Sioux force, however, found it too costly to overrun the scouts who had taken up positions on a small island on the Arickaree branch of the Republican. Less than a month later, Major William B. Royall, with three companies of cavalry, drove along the Beaver River of western Kansas looking for Indians. Instead, Tall Bull found him, hitting his camp and killing two troopers while running off twenty-six horses.[25]

Sheridan led another force into Indian Territory in November. There Custer struck and destroyed Black Kettle's village of Cheyennes on the Washita River. Though some of the Cheyennes, such as Chief Little Robe, decided there was no choice but to go in to the reservation, Tall Bull voiced his intention of going north and joining the Sioux. He said that the Cheyennes had always been a free people and that he would rather die than settle down on a reservation. Taking with him some 165 lodges of Dog Soldiers and their families, Tall Bull established a village on the Republican River. In the spring of 1869, Major E. A. Carr attacked the Cheyenne village, killing twenty-five of Tall Bull's five hundred warriors, who fought a delaying battle while the women and children escaped.[26]

The Dogs retaliated for Carr's attack by striking viciously against the frontier settlements of Kansas, killing settlers and taking two white women as prisoners. Under constant harrassment by Carr, however, Tall Bull led his band northward, intending to cross the Platte River, which was then flooded over its banks. Carr followed, guided by scouts from the Cheyennes' enemies, the Pawnees. On July 11, 1869, Carr caught up with Tall Bull near Summit Springs in northeastern Colorado and attacked. During the fight Tall Bull was killed by Major Frank North, commander of the Pawnee scouts. It was reported that Tall Bull killed one of the white women and wounded the other before being killed himself. His village was destroyed with fifty-two Cheyennes killed and seventeen women and children captured. The remnants of the encampment fled northward to the Sioux camps on the White River.[27]

Bull Bear, who had been with the Dog Soldiers in the north, returned to Indian Territory in November, 1869, and joined the Cheyenne villages at Camp Supply. In a council there he requested that Carr release those of his people who were still being held captive.[28] Bull Bear continued to resist reservation captivity for a number of years, however. He again moved northward during the winter of 1870–71, joining the Sioux. But he was back in Indian Territory in the fall of 1871, visiting Quaker agent Brinton Darlington at the new Cheyenne-Arapaho agency on the North Canadian River. Bull Bear was among the first of the Cheyennes to move in close to the agency and to place his children in the schools of the whites.[29]

During the fall of 1872 a surveying party in southern Kansas on Crooked Creek was visited by a party of Cheyennes under Bull Bear and Big Jake. The Indians greeted them in a friendly fashion, as the *Kansas Daily Tribune* reported:

> Bull Bear was dressed in the usual Indian costume, and wore a large medal of silver, on one side bearing the word "Andrew Johnson, President of the United States," and on the other side, a white man and an Indian shaking hands, with the word "Peace" in a wreathe over their heads. He was a very tall man—fully six feet six inches, and very large otherwise. A few gray hairs were scattered through his hair; but his face was not wrinkled, his eye dimmed nor his natural strength abated. He was a man, in the true sense of the word. He rode into camp one evening with a fine morocco port manteau, which he opened and showed us his papers, which said that he was a good Indian, which he proved himself to be. He,

however, did not like to have the land surveyed. He put his hands on the ground about two feet apart, then raising them about a foot and a half, and then bringing them together he said:

"No good."

He referred to the pits and mounds of the section, and quarter section corners. He said that when he was at Washington they gave him all the lands south of the Arkansas river, and he would like to have us leave, but would not hurry us away. He gave us ten day's stay in his country. This suited us very well, as we could do our work in six days, so we accepted the treaty, and all smoked the pipe of peace with him. He took supper with us, and I spread down my blankets and his together, and we "bunked" together for the night.[30]

Tall Bull had died the defiant death of a Dog Soldier. But Bull Bear, warrior though he was, had always been more of a peace chief. The Reverend Robert Hamilton met Bull Bear at a Baptist Sunday meeting near Kingfisher Creek and found him to be "a man of pleasing and commanding appearance."[31] Bull Bear told the minister he was glad he had come among the Cheyennes for the Jesus religion was useless to the Indians without a good guide.

In 1889 the famous western artist Frederick Remington visited Darlington Agency. He mentioned one old Indian he saw there: "His name is Bull Bear, and he was a strange object with many wrinkles, gray hair, and toothless jaws."[32] Remington did not know he had met one of the greatest leaders of the Cheyenne Nation.

ROMAN NOSE

Roman Nose[33] was not a Cheyenne peace chief—George Bent makes this point on several occasions—but he was an outstanding warrior of the tribe. Moreover, he so epitomized the Cheyenne warrior that even today his name symbolizes the fierce, proud spirit of the Cheyennes. He was also noted for two other distinctions: he was a superb specimen of Cheyenne manhood, and he was killed in one of the classic battles of the American West. Actually there were several Indians among the Plains tribes whose eaglelike countenance caused them to be dubbed "Roman Nose" by the whites. It is not clear, for instance, whether the celebrated Cheyenne warrior was the same man who visited with Governor John Evans at Denver in November, 1863.[34] Evans identified the man as a Northern Arapaho, but the closeness of the two tribes may have led to confusion on Evans' part.

Roman Nose was among the Cheyennes with whom a council was held at Fort Ellsworth in 1866. He was so prominent that Agent Wynkoop reported him as "the head chief of the Northern Band of Cheyennes."[35] A General Rodenbough who was present at the council penned a description of the impressive warrior:

> Roman Nose moved in a solemn and majestic manner to the centre of the chamber. He was one of the finest specimens of the untamed savage. It would be difficult to exaggerate in describing his superb physique. A veritable man of war, the shock of battle and scenes of carnage and cruelty were as the breath of his nostrils; about thirty years of age, standing six feet three inches high, he towered, giant-like, above his companions. A grand head, with strongly marked features, lighted by a pair of fierce black eyes; a large mouth with thin lips, through which gleamed rows of strong white teeth; a Roman nose, with delicate nostrils like those of a thoroughbred horse, first attracted attention, while a broad chest, with symmetrical limbs, on which the muscles under the bronze of his skin stood out like twisted wire, were some of the points of this splendid animal. Clad in buckskin leggings and moccasins, elaborately embroidered with beads and feathers, with a single eagle feather in his scalp-lock, and that rarest of robes, a *white* buffalo, beautifully tanned and as soft as cashmere, thrown over his naked shoulders, he stood forth, the war-chief of the Cheyennes."[36]

Harper's Weekly reporter, Theodore Davis, who encountered Roman Nose at the Pawnee Fork with the Hancock expedition, was similarly struck by the Cheyenne:

> I have never seen so fine a specimen of the Indian race as he—quite six feet in height and finely-formed ... dressed in the uniform of a United States officer, and provided with a numerous quantity of arms, he rode his well-formed pony up to Hancock and proposed to talk. From his manner it was quite evident that he was indifferent whether he talked or fought. His carbine, a Spencer, hung at the side of his pony, four heavy revolvers were stuck in his belt, while his left hand grasped a bow and a number of arrows— the bow being strung and ready for instant use.[37]

George Bent and Roman Nose belonged to the same Crooked Lance society and knew each other well. Bent said that as a boy Roman Nose was called by the name of Sautie, or the Bat, and as he grew into a warrior his name was changed to Waquini, or Hook Nose, which the whites changed to Roman Nose. Bent also described the warrior as being "strong as a bull, tall even for a Cheyenne, broad-shouldered and deep-chested" and said that he was in the prime of his life when he was killed on the Arickaree.[38]

Roman Nose was a Northern Cheyenne who became prominent during the great Cheyenne-Sioux raids following the Sand Creek Massacre. One of the first important battles against the whites in which Roman Nose is known to have participated was the Platte Bridge fight of July, 1865, in which Lieutenant Caspar Collins was killed. As one of the warrior leaders, Roman Nose, fully war-bonneted and armed mostly with bow and arrows, helped lead a charge against a small army wagon train under Collins' escort of twenty-five men.[39]

Barely a month later a huge combined force of Southern Cheyennes, Northern Cheyennes, Arapahoes, and Sioux attacked a detachment of soldiers on the Powder River, and once again Roman Nose played a major role. Leading a massed charge on the troops, the Cheyenne rode the entire length of the line of firing troops, his long war bonnet trailing almost to the ground even on his white war pony. The troops fired on him with rifles and even howitzers as Roman Nose made three or four sweeps, daringly ever closer to them, until finally a shot struck the pony and knocked it from under Roman Nose. He escaped unharmed, however.[40]

When the Dog Soldiers moved back south of the Platte River during 1866, Roman Nose went with them.[41] He was thus present at Fort Ellsworth where annuity goods were distributed by the Indian agent in August and where Rodenbough saw him. Three months later, on November 10, 1866, Roman Nose attended a council held at Fort Zarah, Kansas, with Captain Charles Bogy. Bogy said that he was there to get the Indians to sign the amendments to the Treaty of the Little Arkansas and to hear their complaints. Roman Nose was not at all reluctant to state his mind:

I have made peace with the troops in the North (meaning Fort Laramie). I did not come here for a coat or something to eat. I came here to listen to what you have to say about the killings of the white man (Mexican). If I talked all day the whites would pay no attention to it. I do not believe the whites. I do not love them. If I had plenty of warriors I would drive them out of this country. But we are weak. The whites are strong. We cannot count them. We must listen to what they say. At the treaty made at the North, the Commissioners did not speak of making roads on the Smoky Hill. Our nation is not properly represented here; therefore we should not speak for them. . . .

We made peace on the North Fork of the Platte. We have kept it. Everytime we meet the whites in council, we have new men to talk to us. They have new roads to open. We do not like it. I did not come here to represent myself as a chief but as a soldier.[42]

Roman Nose was in the Cheyenne-Sioux camp on the Pawnee Fork when Hancock arrived on April 12, 1867, with his Indian-hunting expedition, including the Seventh Cavalry under Lieutenant Colonel George Armstrong Custer. Not being a chief, Roman Nose was not with Bull Bear and the rest of the Cheyenne delegation that visited Hancock at his tent. But when Hancock and Custer began their march toward the Indian village, they suddenly came face to face with a long battle line of fully armed, painted, and battle-ready Cheyenne and Sioux warriors who blocked Hancock's advance. At their head, in all his plumed magnificence, was the warrior of warriors, Roman Nose. Though they were greatly outnumbered by the soldiers, there was no doubt that the Indians were prepared to do battle. Custer's Seventh Cavalry, freshly organized, along with infantry and artillery units, whipped about into formation facing the Indians.

Through the efforts of Agent Wynkoop, a parley was arranged. Led by Roman Nose, the Cheyenne delegation met Hancock, Custer, and their staff officers halfway between the lines of the two armies. Hancock, a tall and handsome man with an excellent Civil War record, knew virtually nothing of Indians. Thinking Roman Nose to be a chief, he was miffed because the warrior had not been with the Cheyenne delegation that had visited him. Now Hancock spurred his horse up to the big Cheyenne and, through an interpreter, demanded to know if the Indians wanted war. Roman Nose replied that if he wanted war, he would not have come so close to the big guns of the soldiers.[43] Hancock broke off the meeting by saying it was too windy to talk in the open, and he stated his intention of moving up near the Indian village and making camp.

The Indians immediately retreated to their village, now suspecting more than ever that Hancock intended to surround them and make an attack, as Chivington had done at Sand Creek. Roman Nose was very angry, and he announced that he would ride out and kill Hancock in front of his troops. "This officer," he said, "is spoiling for a fight. I will kill him in front of his own men and give them something to fight about."[44] But Bull Bear and the other chiefs were fearful that Roman Nose would start a fight that would result in the annihilation of the village. Bull Bear and Tall Bull went with Roman Nose when Hancock, learning that some of the villagers were fleeing the camp, demanded another interview with the leaders. According to Edmond Guerrier, the mixed blood interpreter who was related to Roman Nose by marriage, the Cheyenne warrior was prevented from killing Hancock only when Bull Bear grabbed his bridle and led his horse away.[45]

The Indians of the village made good their escape, leaving their lodges standing. In their wily fashion, Roman Nose and the others led Custer and the Seventh Cavalry on trails that divided, redivided, and finally vanished into the vastness of the Kansas prairie. In frustration, Hancock put the torch to the deserted Indian village, despite the strenuous objections of Agent Wynkoop. But the matter was far from ended or forgotten for Roman Nose. He erroneously blamed Wynkoop, who had invited the chiefs in for the Hancock council and whom Roman Nose had asked to explain matters to Hancock.

Roman Nose was active in raids along the Smoky Hill River during the summer of 1867, and was even reported killed on one occasion. But he was very much alive and formidable that fall, when preliminary talks were being held with the Cheyennes at Medicine Lodge Creek by Indian Superintendent Thomas Murphy. When Roman Nose learned that Wynkoop was with Murphy, he and ten other Cheyennes made a dash on the camp.[46] There is little doubt that Wynkoop would have been killed and scalped had he not made a run for Fort Larned. It is also significant that Roman Nose was one of the few prominent

Cheyennes who refused to attend the Medicine Lodge council.

When war on the plains erupted following the Saline and Solomon raids of August, 1868, the Dog Soldiers faded back into their stronghold in the untamed country of the Upper Republican River of northwestern Kansas and northeastern Colorado Territory. Into the very heart of this region Major George Forsyth foolishly led his small band of fifty-three civilian scouts in mid-September. As they advanced deeper and deeper into the Indian country, crossing the Kansas line as they followed an Indian trail along the Arickaree branch of the Republican, the Indian signs became more and more evident. But Forsyth refused to listen to the words of caution from Lieutenant Fred Beecher, second in command, or the head scout, Sharp Grover. The trail that Forsyth was following led to a large encampment of Dog Soldiers, Sioux, and a few Arapahoes, under Bull Bear, Tall Bull, and White Horse. Roman Nose also was there.

On the afternoon of September 16, the Forsyth scouts went into camp on the Arickaree's north bank. They were spotted by braves, who reported their presence to the Dog Soldier camp. Immediately criers began making their rounds of the villages, haranguing the fighting men. Warriors quickly donned their war paint and gear, and on the morning of the seventeenth a large force of Indians attacked Forsyth's band just as the scouts were making ready to break camp.

Roman Nose was not among the original attackers. During a feast that the Cheyennes had given for the Sioux a few days before, a taboo against the use of metal eating tools had been unwittingly broken when a Sioux squaw took bread from a skillet for Roman Nose with an iron fork. When he learned of the infraction later, Roman Nose felt that his battle medicine was so weakened that he might be killed if he went into battle that day.[47]

When attacked, the Forsyth scouts immediately took refuge on a small sandbar in the nearly dry bed of the Arickaree, leaving behind their pack mules with the few rations they had left. Tying their horses to the scattered bushes and willows on the island, the scouts took up positions in a defensive circle. The Indians made the first charge against the island at around nine o'clock that morning. A wall of fire from the scouts halted it short at mid-stream. During the charge Indian sharpshooters poured bullets into the fortifications and took a deadly toll of the officers. Forsyth was hit in the right thigh, and another shot shattered his left leg. Lieutenant Beecher was hit also twice, one of the bullets mortally wounding him in the spine. Acting Surgeon J. H. Mooers was wounded in the head, dying three days later without regaining consciousness.

At eleven o'clock the Indians launched a second charge, but now the men on the island had dug into the sandy soil and, with better breastworks, presented even more effective counterfire. The charge of the Indians was again halted, and the warriors dashed sullenly back out of reach of the rifle fire. Almost immediately a third charge was made, but it was clear that the determination of the braves was weakening. Now the sharpshooters began shooting for the picketed horses of the scouts, picking them off one by one until the last animal squealed in agony and fell thrashing to the ground.

During a lull in the fighting a chief was seen on an elevation near the island and was heard to address his men by saying, "Young warriors, we are many and the whites are few. The whites' bullets are almost all gone. All now that is needed is one big run to bring the whites in." The brave whooped at the words of the chief, but when they had quieted Grover shouted out to the chief, "Hello, old fellow, what do you think now? This is pretty tough, ain't it?" The chief supposedly looked in the direction of the island and replied, "You speak right straight."[48] The chief was probably a Sioux, for Grover knew the Sioux tongue best.

The younger braves were becoming discouraged, and Bull Bear and White Horse sent word back to the Dog Soldier camp for Roman Nose, asking for his help in leading the dispirited young men in another charge. Even though he felt that his weakened medicine could well bring about his death, Roman Nose could not refuse the call to battle. Wearing his famous one-horned war bonnet, he rode to the battlefield. The arrival of this reowned warrior caused a great deal of excitement among the young braves, and one more big charge was planned for the day, which was now reaching late afternoon.

At sunset the final charge was made with Roman Nose at the lead. A hail of bullets buzzed by the Cheyenne as he spurred his war-horse down the bed of the stream toward the island. He was unaware that one of the scouts had taken up a position in some tall grass at one end of the island. As he passed the main body of scouts, Roman Nose was struck in the back by a bullet from the lone sniper. The warrior did not fall from his horse but rode back to where the other Indians were and lay down on the ground. When Bull Bear and White Horse came up, he told them he had been shot. He was later taken back to the main village by the women and died there the next morning.[49]

For a time the whites did not know whom they had killed in the fight. After the Indians had drifted away, help finally reached the beleaguered party of scouts on September 25. The relief column discovered several Indians buried on scaffolds. One of them wore a headdress "composed of buckskin beautifully beaded and ornamented, with a polished buffalo horn on the frontal part and eagle feathers down the back."[50] George Bent later claimed that this dead Indian was a Sioux and not Roman Nose, but he did not say where Roman Nose was buried.[51]

8

The Great Peacemaker

Black Kettle

*We have come with our eyes shut . . . like coming
through the fire. . . . we have been travelling through a
cloud; the sky has been dark ever since the war
began. . . . I have not come here with a little wolf's
bark, but have come to talk plain with you.*

Black Kettle

Without doubt the most significant and famous Cheyenne chief
of all was Black Kettle,[1] the peacemaker chief. Possessing the
wisdom of Yellow Wolf, Old Tobacco, and other peace chiefs,
Black Kettle attempted to guide the Cheyennes through the
difficult years of frontier conflict between 1860 and 1868. His
village twice massacred by United States troops at Sand Creek
and the Washita, himself disgraced among his own people for
leading them into the Sand Creek betrayal and vilified by white
military leaders in order to justify their acts of war, Black Kettle
played a tragic role in the cause of peace between the Cheyennes
and the whites.

There are conflicting accounts of Black Kettle's early life.
General William S. Harney, when he attended the Medicine
Lodge council in 1867, claimed that he had first met the
Cheyenne chief forty-two years earlier at the mouth of the
Teton River with Atkinson. Harney told reporters that in 1825
he had adopted Black Kettle, the son of High-Backed Wolf, as
his own son. "The General brought him down some fine pre-
sents and the Black Kettle pays the General profound def-
erence."[2] Harney's claim was supported by Major Edward
Wynkoop, who knew Black Kettle well, in an address to the
United States Indian Commission:

> To conclude by answering your questions in regard to my
> knowledge of Black Kettle, who has recently been killed in the
> attack upon his village on the Washita River, I would state that

Black Kettle was 56 years of age at the time of his death. He was the son of High Back Wolf, once a principal chief of the Cheyenne nation, and the particular friend of Gen. Harney, who many years ago took considerable interest in the boy Black Kettle. Upon the death of High Back Wolf, his son Black Kettle succeeded him, and soon, by means of his administrative ability and wisdom, rather than by deeds of prowess in the field, became a great chieftain. He was not only regarded as the ruling spirit of his tribe, but was also looked upon by all nomadic tribes of the Plains as a superior, one whose word was law, whose advice was to be heeded. His innate dignity and lofty bearing, combined with his sagacity and intelligence, had that moral effect which placed him in the position of a potentate. The whole force of his nature was concentrated in the one idea of how best to act for the good of his race; he knew the power of the white man, and was aware that thence might spring most of the evils that could befall his people, and consequently the whole of his powers were directed toward conciliating the whites, and his utmost endeavors used to preserve peace and friendship between his race and their oppressors.[3]

George Bent, however, who was married to Black Kettle's niece claimed that Black Kettle was sixty-one years old when he died[4] and that he was the son of Swift Hawk Lying Down, who was never a chief. Black Kettle, Bent stated, was a member of the Sutaio tribe, which joined with the Cheyennes from the northeast and spoke much the same language. The Sutaios camped apart from the Cheyennes for a time, but during the late eighteenth century they became one of the tribal divisions.[5] After his first wife was lost to the Utes, Black Kettle married into the Wotapio division and, according to tribal custom, went to live with his wife's people.[6]

Not much is known about Black Kettle as a young man. George Bent described him as a good warrior and said he was among the Cheyenne scouts who located the Kiowa camp on Wolf Creek in 1838. In 1848, Black Kettle led an expedition against the Utes, taking along his first wife who was captured.[7] Grinnell wrote that Black Kettle carried the sacred Medicine Arrows into battle against the Delawares in 1853,[8] and Bent listed him as one of the chiefs who were on the Smoky Hill River when Sumner led his saber attack against the Cheyennes in 1857.[9]

Bent claimed that Black Kettle became a chief when Old

Bark, or Bear's Feather, died.[10] He gave the date as 1850, but Bark was alive and present at the Fort Laramie treaty revision of 1853; so it must be assumed the date is in error. Though the Harney-Wynkoop version of Black Kettle's parentage and history is questionable on some counts, the possibility of his being the son of High-Backed Wolf might explain the occasional mention of the latter name following the chief's death in 1834. By this logic, the "High-Backed-Wolf" who appeared at Bent's place in October, 1857, in the company of White Antelope, Tall Bear, and Lean Bear might actually have been Black Kettle, who is known to have been a principal chief in 1860.

The first historical evidence of Black Kettle by his accepted name was in 1860, when Commissioner A. B. Greenwood met the Cheyenne chiefs at Fort Wise to conduct a treaty council.[11] From then until his death, Black Kettle was clearly, as Cheyenne squawman John Prowers put it, *the* principal man of the tribe, even when in disfavor with the warring element.[12] Agent Albert G. Boone, who completed the Fort Wise treaty with the Cheyennes after Greenwood left, found that only Black Kettle could fully comprehend the details of matters under consideration.[13] Black Kettle was the first signer to the treaty for the Cheyennes.

When Governor Evans dispatched Elbridge Gerry to meet with the Cheyennes in 1863, Gerry reported that the war chiefs claimed the treaty was a swindle and that Black Kettle and White Antelope denied signing it.[14] This report was probably a lie fabricated either by the Dog Soldiers or by Gerry, for Black Kettle never otherwise made such a denial, and he was ever willing to make peace with the whites. Such was the case when Lean Bear was murdered on the Smoky Hill River. According to an account given to George Bent by Wolf Chief, Black Kettle did all he could to stop the fighting after Lean Bear had been shot.[15]

Black Kettle's desire for harmony between his people and the whites was also apparent in the letter he sent in to Fort Lyon to bring about an end to the conflict that erupted on the central plains during the summer of 1864. With the help of George Bent, Black Kettle wrote:

Cheyenne Village, August 29, 1864

We received a letter from Bent, wishing us to make peace. We

106

held a council in regard to it; all come to the conclusion to make peace with you, providing you make peace with the Kiowas, Comanches, Arapahoes, Apaches, and Sioux. We are going to send a messenger to the Kiowas and to the other nations about our going to make peace with you. We heard that you have some prisoners at Denver; we have some prisoners of yours which we are willing to give up, providing you give up yours. There are three war parties out yet, and two of Arapahoes; they have been out some time and expected in soon. When we held this council there were a few Arapahoes and Sioux present. We want true news from you in return. (That is a letter.)

BLACK KETTLE and other Chiefs[16]

The letter was carried by subchief One Eye, who offered himself and his wife as hostages if Major Wynkoop, then commanding Fort Lyon, would go to talk with Black Kettle and the other chiefs. When Wynkoop appeared on the Smoky Hill River with his garrison force and two howitzers, the Dog Soldiers were greatly excited, fearing another attack such as Lieutenant George S. Eayre had made. They demanded to know why, if Wynkoop wanted peace, he had brought his men and guns. Wynkoop replied that he had brought only a few men in case of trouble with bad Indians. Further, he said, he was not a big enough chief to make peace, but if the Indians would give up their white captives he would do his utmost to reestablish good relations with the Indians.[17]

Some of the Dog Soldiers were still very angry, saying that Wynkoop was treating them like fools or children in asking them to give up captives, for which they had given many horses and buffalo robes, and offering nothing in return. When one chief suggested that the Indians attack the troops, One Eye stood up and vehemently offered his defense of Wynkoop, saying he would fight on the side of the soldiers if there was trouble.[18] Wynkoop described Black Kettle's response:

> During this whole time the head Chief Black Kettle had remained as immovable as a statue, but he now quietly said a few words to One-Eye, who retired; then waved his hand and "silence fell." He arose, gathered his blankets around him, advanced to where I was and took me by the hand, afterwards embraced me twice and led me to the center of the Council ring; remaining by my side he addressed the assembled Chiefs with words to this effect:

Delegation of chiefs at Denver in September, 1864. *Seated, left to right:*
Bull Bear, Black Kettle, Arapaho chief Neva, and White Antelope.
"Black Kettle was not a hostile and never had been; his boast was that
his hand had never been raised against a white man, woman, or child.
. . . He was a mild, peaceable, pleasant, good man."—J. R. Mead, *Wichita
Eagle. Courtesy of Denver Public Library Western Collection.*

"This white man is not here to laugh at us, nor does he regard us
as children, but on the contrary unlike the balance of his race, he
comes with confidence in the pledges given by the Red Man. He
had been told by one of our bravest warriors, that he should come
and go unharmed, he did not close his ears, but with his eyes shut
followed on the trail of him whom we had sent as our messenger.

108

It was like coming through the fire, for a white man to follow and believe in the words of one of our race, whom they have always branded as unworthy of confidence or belief. He has not come with a forked tongue or with two hearts, but his words are straight and his heart single. Had he told us that he would give us peace, on the condition of our delivering to him the white prisoners, he would have told us a lie. For I know that he cannot give us peace, there is a greater Chief in the far off camp of the white soldiers, who must talk to one even still mightier, to our Great Father in Washington who must tell his soldiers to bury the hatchet, before we can again roam over the Prairies in safety and hunt the buffalo. Had this white soldier come to us with crooked words, I myself would have despised him; and would have asked whether he thought we were fools, that he could sing sweet words into our ears, and laugh at us when we believed them. But he has come with words of truth; and confidence, in the pledges of his Red brothers, and whatever be the result of these deliberations, he shall return unharmed to his lodge from whence he came. It is I Moka-ta-va-tah that says it."[19]

Wynkoop described the Cheyenne principal chief as "one who had stamped on every lineament, the fact that he was born to command, he while all the balance of the council were snarling like wolves, sat calm, dignified, immovable with a slight smile on his face."[20] An agreement was reached whereby Wynkoop would wait three or four days while the white prisoners, some of which were with the Sioux, were obtained. The Sioux, Black Kettle said, did not want peace with the whites, and it would be difficult to secure their release.[21]

Even within his own tribe, Black Kettle had no authority to procure the captives without following Cheyenne custom and buying them. Using his own ponies, Black Kettle purchased the freedom of four white children and delivered them to Wynkoop: Laura Roper, a sixteen- or seventeen-year-old girl who had been captured on the Blue River in Kansas along with two other children; Daniel Marble, age seven or eight; Isabel Ewbanks, a four- or five-year-old child whose mother had cut her dress into strips and hanged herself while in captivity; and Ambrose Archer, a seven- or eight-year-old who said he would just as lief stay with the Indians as not.[22]

Wynkoop then escorted a delegation of three Cheyennes— Black Kettle, White Antelope, and Bull Bear—and four Arapaho chiefs to Denver for a council with Governor Evans, meeting at Denver's Camp Weld on September 28, 1864. Upon Evans' request that the Cheyenne speak first, Black Kettle opened the council with a short speech, admitting there were still two women and a child out. He said they would be delivered up as soon as he could secure their release. Through interpreter John Simpson Smith, Black Kettle told Evans:

> I followed Major Wynkoop to Fort Lyon, and Major Wynkoop proposed that we come up to see you. We have come with our eyes shut, following his handful of men, like coming through the fire. All we ask is that we may have peace with the whites; we want to hold you by the hand. You are our father; we have been travelling through a cloud; the sky has been dark ever since the war began. These braves who are with me are all willing to do what I say. We want to take good tidings home to our people, that they may sleep in peace. I want you to give all the chiefs of the soldiers here to understand that we are for peace. and that we have made peace, that we may not be mistaken by them for enemies. I have not come here with a little wolf's bark, but have come to talk plain with you. We must live near the buffalo or starve. When we came here we came free, without any apprehension, to see you, and when I go home and tell my people that I have taken your hand and the hands of all the chiefs here in Denver, they will feel well, and so will all the different tribes of Indians on the plains, after we have eaten and drunk with them.[23]

But Black Kettle's pleas for understanding had little effect. Evans began an interrogation designed to make the Indians admit their guilt for starting the war. He made no effort to reconcile differences and bring an end to the war but instead accused the Cheyennes and Arapahoes of forming an alliance with the Sioux. The governor was still annoyed because they had refused to talk peace with him when he had sent Gerry out to see them. Evans told the chiefs that soon the war between the whites would be over and that the plains would swarm with United States soldiers. He ended by saying that his best advice to the chiefs would be to help the army, and Black Kettle said that they were willing to do that.[24]

Upon returning to the prairie, Black Kettle led a party of principal men to Fort Lyon, where he discovered that Wynkoop had been replaced in command of the fort by Major Scott J. Anthony, a fellow officer to Wynkoop in the Colorado First Cavalry. In a council with the Cheyenne men, Anthony told them that since he could not issue them rations—there was already an outbreak of scurvy at Lyon—they should remain at their encampment on the big bend of Sand Creek some forty miles above the fort. There the young men of the village could go hunting, and they would be perfectly safe from United States troops, Anthony said. Black Kettle, understanding the ration problem, said that he was satisfied with that arrangement, and, after visiting his old friend William Bent, he led his band back to the Sand Creek village. The Indians did not really trust the "Red-Eye" chief, Anthony, but there was little choice when he vowed to support Wynkoop's peace policies.[25]

At dawn on the morning of November 28, 1864, Colonel Chivington, willingly supported by Major Anthony, attacked the Cheyennes at Sand Creek. According to George Bent and others who were in the Cheyenne camp at the time, Black Kettle was notified by a squaw that troops were approaching along the river from the south. Not knowing where the troops came from but fearing they might be General James Blunt's men from Kansas, Black Kettle went into his lodge and got a large American flag that had been given to him by Greenwood in 1860. With White Antelope's help he tied the flag to the end of a lodge pole along with a white flag and stood waving it in front of his tipi. But the troops commenced firing, surrounding the village. Black Kettle remained there until most of the women and children had fled. But the blue-coated troops continued to pour over and around the low sand hills on the south bank of the creek, and Black Kettle finally took his wife and started up the creek after the others. His wife was hit by a bullet and knocked to the ground. Black Kettle ran back to where she lay on a sandbar, but she appeared to be dead; so he hurried on to where other Cheyennes were hiding under the creek bank. The soldiers came up and shot the Cheyenne woman eight more times, but she miraculously survived the bombardment. When the soldiers withdrew around dusk, Black Kettle returned and carried his wife off to the Dog Soldier camps on the Smoky Hill River.[26]

The massacre of over a hundred Cheyenne villagers, the destruction of the entire accouterments of the camp, and the capture of several hundred Cheyenne horses and mules touched off the powder keg of Dog Soldier hatred and mistrust of the whites. The Dog Soldiers, indifferent to the fact that it had been Colorado whites who massacred the Cheyenne village, ripped up the lines of transportation and frontier settlements throughout Kansas.

Though Black Kettle survived, several Cheyenne chiefs were killed in the slaughter: Standing-in-Water and War Bonnet, who had gone with Lean Bear to Washington in 1863; White Antelope; Yellow Wolf; Knock Knee; and One Eye. Arapaho chief Left Hand, who had been in the Cheyenne camp was also killed. Black Kettle, now in disgrace, took his few remaining followers south of the Arkansas River. In the fall of 1865, a year after the massacre, the peace emissaries for the Little Arkansas council found Black Kettle on the Cimarron River south of Fort Dodge. At the council, Black Kettle told how it was with him now:

The Great Father above hears us, and the Great Father at Washington will hear what we say. Is it true that you came here from Washington, and is it true what you say here to-day? The Big Chief he give his words to me to come and meet here, and I take hold and retain what he says. I believe all to be true, and think it is all true. Their young white men, when I meet them on the plains, I give them my horse and my moccasins, and I am glad to-day to think that the Great Father has sent good men to take pity on us. Your young soldiers I don't think they listen to you. You bring presents, and when I come to get them I am afraid they will strike me before I get away. When I come in to receive presents I take them up crying. Although wrongs have been done me I live in hopes. I have not got two hearts. These young men, (Cheyennes) when I call them into the lodge and talk with them, they listen to me and mind what I say. Now we are again together to make peace. My shame (mortification) is as big as the earth, although I will do what my friends advise me to do. I once thought that I was the only man that persevered to be the friend of the white man, but since they have come and cleaned out (robbed) our lodges, horses, and everything else, it is hard for me to believe white men any more. Here we are, altogether, Arrapahoes and Cheyennes, but few of us, we are one people. As soon as you arrived you started runners after us and the Arapahoes with words that I took hold of immediately on hearing them. From what I can see around me, I feel confident that our Great Father has taken pity on me, and I feel that it is the truth all that has been told me to-day. All my friends—the Indians that are holding back—they are afraid to come in; are afraid they will be betrayed as I have been. I am not afraid of white men, but come and take you by the hand, and am glad to have an opportunity of so doing. These lands that you propose to give us I know nothing about. There is but a handful

112

here now of the Cheyenne nation, and I would rather defer making any permanent treaty until the others come. We are living friendly now.

There are a great many white men. Possibly you may be looking for some one with a strong heart. Possibly you may be intending to do something for me better than I know of.[27]

Black Kettle's wife was brought in, and the commission counted her nine Sand Creek wounds. General Harney presented Black Kettle with a fine bay horse.[28] The treaty, conducted with the help of William Bent and Kit Carson, assigned the Cheyennes and Arapahoes a new reserve area in the northern part of Indian Territory. It was signed for the Cheyennes by Black Kettle, Seven Bulls, Little Robe, Black White Man, Minimic or Eagle's Head, and Bull That Hears at the mouth of the Little Arkansas River, near present Wichita, Kansas, on October 17, 1865.[29]

During the winter of 1865–66, Black Kettle was on Bluff Creek below Fort Dodge with about seventy lodges, and Wynkoop, now the Cheyenne and Arapaho agent, delivered a trainload of annuity goods to him there in February. Through the assistance of John Smith, Wynkoop rescued a white girl, Mary Fletcher, who had been captured by Sand Hill's band of Cheyennes on the North Platte River during the 1865 outbreak.[30]

On August 14, 1866, Black Kettle was among the Cheyenne leaders at Fort Ellsworth. The chiefs asked Wynkoop to secure them six hundred ponies to replace those lost at Sand Creek and to find and return the two Indian children taken captive by Chivington's men.[31] Black Kettle was also present at the ensuing council at Fort Zarah on November 13, 1866, with special agent Charles Bogy. He defended the Cheyennes against charges of depredations in the north:

> The questions you have asked us regarding the killing of two men at Chalk Bluffs and running off stock from Fort Wallace I know nothing about, having never heard of it before. The Sioux have been in stealing our horses and have stolen horses around this place and have probably killed the men and stolen the stock you spoke of. Mr. Smith, your Interpreter, was with us nearly all last summer,—(Mr. Smith stated that he had never heard of these depredations before, except some floating rumors around here) and he knows we are not guilty. I have heard from some of the last

Indians that came in, that the Sioux had taken seven horses from the Smoky Hill and that the Dog-soldiers had taken these from them and were bringing them in. The Sioux have stolen horses from the Cheyennes and the Dog soldiers have recovered them. White Horse, a Cheyenne, went with a party of his men and took seven horses from the Sioux and returned them to the whites, four more horses are still in the possession of the Sioux belonging to the whites. Ever since we crossed here in the summer to go north, Smith has been with us and has been trying to get us to come back. At Fort Ellsworth you promised us to be back in six weeks. We came here and waited until we were tired and then went south. I told Col. Bent and Mr. Smith that I was mad and not to send for me.

Notwithstanding the promises made to me had not been fulfilled when we heard that Commissioners were here and had sent for us, Chiefs and soldiers got on their horses and came to hear what you had to say. It is very hard for us to move so often, and we are without proper clothing. Yet we have come again to see you as you requested. We do not approve of the killing of the white man (Mexican) by one of our foolish young men. We have come here to arrange it in some way. What is right is all we want. The reason why we moved from this place as soon as we did was to get away from trouble. By remaining here we are liable to get into trouble. If all had left when I did the murder would not have occurred. Ever since we made peace last fall at mouth Little Arkansas river we have been promised that when our goods came out, wherever we were or wherever we were directed to go there we were to receive our goods. We did not leave here angry or object to receiving our goods, but left through necessity, hoping that you would have these goods issued to us in our villages according to your promises. The distance is too far for us to come in for our goods. I have never refused to obey your calls and have always come when sent for, but it is hard for us to obey your request to come back without villages to receive our goods at this time. You are here again as a Chief sent here to represent the Great Chief at Washington. Your talk is all good and we are going to listen to you. Will it be true, or as heretofore not come out as you represent it? We will leave once again. There may be some jumping around yet, but we will trust you. Our women and children at this season are not in condition to come here, and if you can take our goods where we are camped, it would be highly helpful.[32]

Black Kettle was south of the Arkansas River on the Cimarron when Hancock had his confrontation with Bull Bear, Tall Bull, and Roman Nose on the Pawnee Fork in the spring of 1867. By the fall of that year he had dropped as far south as the North Fork of the Red River.[33] A courier found Black Kettle's village there and delivered a letter from Colonel Jesse Leavenworth, agent for the Comanches and Kiowas, asking the various tribes to come in for another peace council.

Despite the danger he would face as a result of the recent killing of a Wichita Indian by some Cheyennes, Black Kettle decided to ride up and meet with Leavenworth at the mouth of the Little Arkansas River. George Bent stated that he was with Black Kettle's small party when Leavenworth read a long letter saying that a number of peace commissioners were coming out to make a new peace treaty.[34]

Black Kettle returned to his village and moved it northward to Wolf Creek in northwestern Indian Territory. On September 11, 1867, Leavenworth met with the headmen of the Kiowas, Comanches, and Plains Apaches on the Salt Fork of the Arkansas River. A newspaper correspondent with Leavenworth reported that the Apaches told of Black Kettle's band being "corralled" by the Dog Soldiers, who wanted no peace and would allow no one to leave except those on the warpath. Black Kettle and George Bent, along with Little Raven of the Arapahoes and Poor Bear of the Apaches, had evaded the Dog Soldiers and gone to Fort Larned to talk peace.[35]

Despite the open threats of the Dog Soldiers, Black Kettle agreed that he would attend the treaty council, which was to be held on Medicine Lodge Creek south of Fort Larned. When the peace commission's wagon train arrived there on October 14, they found Black Kettle's village already encamped and waiting. The Cheyenne principal chief rode out to meet the peace commission cortege, and the reporter Stanley described him as wearing "a tall dragoon hat, while flowing over his shoulders, and trailing on the ground, was a long robe of the finest blue cloth."[36] He warned the commissioners that there were over three hundred Dog Soldiers on the Cimarron River to the south and that he could not guarantee they would not attack the camp.[37] In the preliminary meeting Black Kettle had only a few words to say after chiefs of the other tribes had spoken. "We were once friends with the whites," he accused the commissioners, "but you nudged us out of the way by your intrigues."[38]

When Tall Bull, Gray Head, and other Dog Soldier leaders threatened to kill his horses if he did not attend the Medicine

Arrow rites, Black Kettle continued to play the peacemaker. He told the commissioners: "I give you my word I will not ask you to stay here six or seven or eight days. When I look to my left I see you, and that you intend to do right; and when I look to my right I see my men, and know that they intend to do right. I want you both to touch and shake hands."[39]

Two days later a group of horsemen rode into Commission Camp out of a night rainstorm, wet and dripping, to talk with General Harney in his tent. They were Cheyenne chiefs from the Cimarron camps, and they had stopped by Black Kettle's village and brought him with them to talk with the commissioners. They said, however, that they first needed to confer among themselves. Stanley and other reporters watched the group closely. Black Kettle appeared very nervous and uncomfortable with the others. When the Cheyenne conference was over, Black Kettle explained that four more days would be needed to complete the ceremonies. Already weary and impatient, the commissioners were upset but finally agreed to the delay.[40] The correspondents all agreed that Black Kettle had undoubtedly placed himself in grave danger from his own people by holding strongly to his determination to make peace.[41]

The days dragged by monotonously for the whites, and a mounting concern grew over the intentions of the Dog Soldiers. But when the Cheyennes finally did come, Black Kettle was at their lead:

> Five columns of a hundred men each, forty paces apart, dressed in all their gorgeous finery. Crimson blankets about their loins, tall, comb-like headdresses of eagle feathers, variegated shirts, brass chains, sleigh bells, white, red and blue bead-worked moccasins, gleaming tomahawks, made up the personnel of a scene never to be forgotten. Their chief, *Mo-ko-va-ot-o,* or Black Kettle, mounted upon a wiry horse, sprang forward, dressed in a dingy shirt and dingier blanket, his long black hair floating behind him like a bashaw's tail, and waved his hands. In most admirable order they moved by the left flank by divisions; another wave and they marched obliquely across the Neo-contogwa—up to within 50 yards of Commission Camp, where they halted, but still continued their lively exhilarating chant until the Commission appeared in full dress and halted within a few paces of the line.[42]

When the council was convened with the Cheyennes on the following morning, Black Kettle was at the front of the circle as a

116

principal chief, along with Big Jake, Big Head, Tall Bull, and White Horse. But during the council, the only Cheyenne to speak was a little known chief named Buffalo Chief. Buffalo Chief spoke for the Dog Soldiers in saying that the Cheyennes would never give up the country between the Arkansas and South Platte rivers.[43] The chiefs were persuaded to sign the treaty document, which stipulated they give up that land for a reserve in Indian Territory, only when Senator Henderson verbally promised them, contrary to what the treaty said, that they could still roam and hunt there as long as there were buffalo.

Affairs on the Kansas plains were quiet through the winter of 1867–68. Black Kettle's band remained in camps south of the Arkansas River but grew increasingly restless when the government failed to produce the annuity goods that had been promised them at Medicine Lodge. Whisky peddlers from Dodge were active among the tribes, and John Smith warned that it was getting out of hand. Finally in March, 1868, Wynkoop secured an issuance of food stuff and delivered it to the tribes on Bluff Creek. Not included were arms and ammunition, which the Indians said had been promised them at Medicine Lodge, and the Cheyennes claimed they were being cheated again. In May, when the combined Cheyenne and Arapaho force advanced on Council Grove, Kansas, to seek revenge against the Kaws, Black Kettle was not involved.

Another annuity payment was issued to the Cheyennes and Arapahoes at Fort Larned in mid-July, but the Cheyenne Dog Soldiers sullenly refused to take part when they saw that there were still no guns or ammunition. On August 6, 1868, Black Kettle and about 150 men, women, and children appeared at the military post at Fort Hays. He said that he wished to take his village north in search of game and wanted to duly report the matter to the military authorities. He expressed his friendship toward the whites once more and requested and received rations.[44] The Hays City *Advance* reported the event:

A band of Cheyennes under command of Black Kettle, a noted chief, was in town on Thursday. They had a white child with them, which they claimed to be a half-breed, the offspring of an officer at Dodge and a squaw of the tribe. Some think there is no Indian blood in the child, but that it was stolen from Texas by Kiowas or Comanches and sold to the Cheyennes. Anyhow, if it belongs to any of our shoulder-strapped friends at Larned, they shouldn't be ashamed of it. Cheyenne stock is good stock.[45]

As Black Kettle was joining a larger body of Cheyenne Dog Soldiers on the Upper Saline River northwest of Hays, a war party of Sioux, Arapahoes, and Cheyennes—a few of them from Black Kettle's band—headed eastward down the Saline for a raid on the Pawnees. Instead, however, the whisky-drinking party came in conflict with white settlers along the river and committed a series of atrocities in the vicinity of the Saline and Solomon rivers. Several whites were killed, women and children were taken prisoners, and stock was stolen. Coming as this did on the heels of an issuance of guns and ammunition by Wynkoop at Fort Larned on August 9, the two events seemed directly connected in the minds of the Kansas populace and the military, under General Phil Sheridan.

On August 19, 1868, Chief Little Rock, of Black Kettle's band, gave a full and open account of the affair as the Indians knew it to Agent Wynkoop at Fort Larned. He admitted the Cheyennes' guilt and named the ones responsible, including the young men who had slipped away from Black Kettle's village to join the war party.[46] Nevertheless, these depredations now gave the upper hand to the war-minded among the whites and laid the foundation for Sheridan's winter campaign into Indian Territory. They also were the basis for charges by the military that Black Kettle was guilty of acts of war against the whites.

The Cheyenne principal chief now moved his village back into Indian Territory, following the advice of old John Smith that they should avoid possible traps at forts Larned and Cobb. Sheridan later stated that he had issued an invitation to Black Kettle to come in to Larned and talk but that the Cheyenne had refused. Black Kettle had only to remember Sand Creek to have reason to be wary. Sheridan had already talked with the Kiowas about establishing old Fort Cobb as a new agency point under Major General William M. Hazen.

On October 30, Captain Henry Alvord, who had been sent to Cobb to handle matters until Hazen arrived, reported that Black Kettle and his Cheyennes were just north of the Antelope Hills conducting a buffalo hunt with the Comanches and Kiowas. Old Ten Bears of the Comanches had indicated that soon he would escort Black Kettle in for a meeting "to arrange for moving a large portion of the Cheyennes south for lasting peace."[47]

This meeting with General Hazen took place on November 20 at Fort Cobb, Black Kettle speaking for the Cheyennes and Big Mouth for the Arapahoes. Black Kettle explained the situation he faced:

> I always feel well while I am among these Indians—the Caddoes, Wichitas, Wacoes, Keechies, &c.—as I know they are all my friends; and I do not feel afraid to go among the white men, because I feel them to be my friends also. The Cheyennes, when south of the Arkansas, did not wish to return to the north side because they feared trouble there, but were continually told that they had better go there, as they would be rewarded for so doing. The Cheyennes do not fight at all this side of the Arkansas; they do not trouble Texas, but north of the Arkansas, some young Cheyennes were fired upon and then the fight began. I have always done my best to keep my young men quiet, but some will not listen, and since the fighting began I have not been able to keep them all at home. But we want peace, and I would be glad to move all my people down this way; I could then keep them all quietly near camp. My camp is now on the Washita, 40 miles east of the Antelope Hills, and I have there about 180 lodges.
>
> I speak only for my own people; I cannot speak nor control the Cheyennes north of the Arkansas.[48]

Hazen replied that he did not control the soldiers under Sheridan who were then in the field, fighting the Indians, and that Black Kettle must go back to his people and try to make peace with Sheridan if he came. Then, if the Great Father told Hazen to treat Black Kettle's Cheyennes as friendly Indians, they would be accepted on the reservation and cared for. Black Kettle said that he understood, and he returned the hundred or more miles up the Washita River to his camp, where an early winter's snowstorm had struck on the twenty-third.

Black Kettle's village consisted of only some fifty lodges on the far western end of a long series of Comanche, Kiowa, Apache, Arapaho, and other Cheyenne encampments spread along the winding Washita River. Upon reaching his village, Black Kettle held a conference with the other headmen. They decided that the next day, November 27—one day short of the fourth anniversary of Sand Creek—the village would move farther down the river to be among the other tribes for better security. None of the headmen, however, felt there was much chance that the troops would be out in such cold, snowy weather.

They were badly mistaken, for at that moment a force of Seventh United States Cavalry under Lieutenant Colonel George Armstrong Custer was marching headlong through the knee-deep snow toward their village. Custer had left the newly established Camp Supply at the mouth of Wolf Creek on the twenty-third, followed Wolf Creek south and westward, and then cut sharply south toward the Antelope Hills, which marked the South Canadian River's entry into Indian Territory from the Texas Panhandle. There a scouting force under Major Joel Elliott had discovered a Kiowa war party trail that led to the Washita and downriver to Black Kettle's camp. During the night of the twenty-sixth, Custer surrounded the village and waited through the frigid night to make his attack at dawn.

As was the custom for a head chief, Black Kettle had his horse tethered near his lodge. When the attack came, he emerged from his lodge to see a wave of blue-coated troops bearing down on his village. He quickly pulled his wife up behind him on the horse and spurred toward a crossing of the Washita at the east end of the camp, following a trail that led downriver to the other camps. But as they reached the bed of the river, Black Kettle and his wife were met by a volley of bullets from the opposite bank, where Elliott's force had taken up positions during the night. Black Kettle and his wife were knocked from the horse, both falling dead into the icy waters of the Washita River.[49] A short time later, Chief Little Rock was killed just downriver as he tried to fight a delaying action that would allow a small group of Cheyenne women to escape.

Thus died the man Black Kettle, who was probably the greatest of all the Cheyenne peace chiefs. Sheridan would write his obituary by referring to him as "a worn out and worthless old cipher,"[50] while the *New York Times* described him as "one of the most troublesome and dangerous characters on the Plains." Black Kettle, the *Times* editorial said, "was one of the most active chiefs in stirring up the tribes of war."[51]

The charges made against Black Kettle by Sheridan and others, despite their lack of substance, will forever linger over the reputation of the Cheyenne peace leader. But the only valid charge that can be made against Black Kettle is that he could not control his young men. The Cheyenne Nation could produce outstanding men but, as Cheyenne scholar E. Adamson Hoebel put it, the chieftain system had no machinery to enforce laws or discipline within the tribe.[52] The white people's government, unable to control the actions of its soldiers and citizens on the frontier, suffered from precisely the same inadequacy. And it was often the peace chiefs, such as Black Kettle and Lean Bear, who perished in the resulting crossfire.

Dull Knife, Northern Cheyenne chief. *Courtesy of National Archives.*

9

Chiefs of the North

Dull Knife, Little Wolf, Little Chief

Great Grandfather sends death in that letter. You will have to kill us and take our bodies back down that trail. We will not go.

Dull Knife

Dull Knife, and Little Wolf and Little Chief were Northern Cheyenne chiefs whose lives followed much the same path. Together they led their people in a historic march from exile in Indian Territory back to their homeland along the Bighorn, Rosebud, Tongue, and Powder rivers. The Northern Cheyennes held a great love for this land, and neither bullets, nor imprisonment, nor freezing cold, nor starvation could kill it.

While their brother bands had drifted south to range over the rolling grassland prairies between the Platte and the Arkansas rivers, the Northern tribesmen had remained in the north in company with the much larger Sioux Nation. Over the years they took on much of the Sioux culture and dress, and even their language began to differ from that of the Southern bands. There was some intercourse between the two divisions of the tribe, but the people of the north preferred the high plains and did not like the south, where the air was heavy and hot.

Dull Knife was known as a brave man and a good fighter, but he was not a good planner and organizer of battles. Little Wolf, on the other hand, always planned his fights carefully in advance. When he was a soldier chief, he had a reputation for never sending anyone ahead of him and often counted the first coup.[1] Little Chief was much more of a politician, demanding justice from the white man for his people but refusing to go to war.

Dull Knife,[2] whose real name was Morning Star, received his nickname when a brother-in-law once chided him for never having a sharp knife. Okohm-ha-ka, usually given as "Little Wolf," is

123

more properly translated as "Little Coyote."[3] Both chiefs initially appear in the historical records in 1856 in connection with an incident at the Upper Platte Bridge some 125 miles above Fort Laramie, the first significant conflict between the Cheyennes and United States troops.

Reports had reached the commandant of Fort Laramie, Major William Hoffman, that a village of Cheyennes encamped near the bridge had in its possession four stray horses belonging to the whites. Hoffman sent word to the village that the horses would have to be brought in. Four Cheyennes, one of them Little Wolf, came in to the post to talk about it. They brought with them three of the four disputed horses, but Little Wolf claimed that the Cheyennes had found the fourth horse in another part of the country much earlier than it was supposed to have been lost. He refused to give it up.[4]

Angered at this insubordination by an Indian, Hoffman issued orders for the four Cheyennes to be placed under arrest. The Cheyennes, thinking they were to be killed, broke and ran. One brave was killed, and one named Wolf Fire was captured, but Little Wolf and the other escaped. The Cheyenne village fled into the hills. On the way, an old trapper named Ganier was killed by two Cheyennes in revenge for the killing of their brave. Later Hoffman held an interview with Chief Dull Knife, who asked for the release of Wolf Fire and promised to turn over the two men who killed the trapper. However, nothing was resolved, and Wolf Fire was held in irons in the Fort Laramie guardhouse. Indian Agent Thomas Twiss tried to secure the release of the Indian, but Hoffman would not set him free. Wolf Fire eventually died in the post stockade, even though Chief White Crow brought in a white boy who had been captured by the Dog Soldiers.[5]

Ten years later Dull Knife played a part in the famous Fetterman Massacre of December 21, 1866. The United States government had wanted to make a new peace with the Sioux and the Northern Cheyennes to ensure protection for the Bozeman Trail, which led northwestward across Wyoming. E. B. Taylor of the Indian Office was sent to Fort Laramie to arrange an agreement. Many of the hostile Sioux did not come to the peace council, despite promises of guns and ammunition as presents. When those attending discovered that even then Colonel Henry

Little Wolf, Northern Cheyenne chief. *Courtesy of National Archives.*

B. Carrington was leading an infantry regiment to build a fort in the Powder River country, they stormed out of the council.[6] George Bent stated that Dull Knife signed the agreement at Fort Laramie and that other Cheyennes were very angry with him and threatened to depose him. Dull Knife claimed that he had been deceived by the interpreters at the council—and there is evidence that Taylor was trying to fool the chiefs—but the Cheyenne leader never fully regained the great prestige he had once known.[7]

Carrington arrived on Big Piney Creek in northern Wyoming, just east of the Big Horn Mountains, with some seven hundred troops of the Twenty-seventh Infantry in June, 1866. He immediately began construction of Fort Phil Kearny, a military post to protect the white transportation on the Bozeman road. When he received a note from Cheyenne Chief Black Horse asking if he wanted peace or war, Carrington invited the Cheyennes to come in for a council. On July 16 the tribe arrived in full dress, led by Black Horse, Dull Knife, and others representing some 167 lodges.[8] The Cheyennes listened to Carrington's request that they side with the whites against the Sioux, but they made no promises. They said only that if the whites advanced no farther they could remain there unmolested so far as they were concerned. But they could not fight against the Sioux; they were too many and the Cheyennes too few.

After leaving Carrington the Cheyennes encamped on Reno Creek, where a large war party of Sioux met them and demanded to know what had gone on between the Cheyennes and the white soldiers. Black Horse told them that the meeting had been friendly, that they had received presents and could get many more by going to Fort Laramie and touching the pen to the white man's paper. The Sioux were infuriated. They had been sitting in a circle glowering at the Cheyennes. Now they jumped to their feet and used their bows to strike the Cheyenne chiefs across their faces and backs, crying "Coup! coup!" as against an enemy in battle. It was an enormous insult for the Cheyenne chiefs, who had never been treated so before, but the Sioux were too strong to fight against.[9] The Cheyennes knew that if they wished to stay in the northern country they loved, they had to remain on the side of the much larger Sioux Nation.

Both Dull Knife and Little Wolf were present that December

126

when Captain William Fetterman and eighty-one officers and men were cut off from Fort Phil Kearny and massacred by a combined force of Cheyennes, Sioux, and Arapahoes. Grinnell, who was later taken over the battlefield by a Cheyenne participant, stated that Dull Knife was one of the leaders of the Cheyenne war parties that helped to lure Captain Fetterman and his troops away from the frontier post.[10] He also cited Cheyenne White Elk, who told of Little Wolf's role in the affair:

> That night the names of ten young were called out, and those called were ordered to start that night and be ready the next morning to attack the post. There were two Cheyennes, two Arapahoes, and two from each of the three tribes of the Sioux who were present. The two Cheyennes were Little Wolf and Wolf Left Hand. After he had been chosen, Little Wolf rode over to the fire at which his brother, Big Nose, was sitting. A few days before, the two brothers had quarrelled with each other. Little Wolf [wishing to do him a great honor] said to his brother: "Brother, I have been called to go and attack the post; take my horse and do you go." Big Nose was still angry and said: "Take back your horse; I do not want him." Bull Hump, who wished to make the brothers friends again, said to Big Nose: "My friend, here are my moccasins and my war clothes. If you have any bad feelings you may have those clothes to lie in." ("To lie in" is to be killed in.) Big Nose accepted the clothes and agreed to go. Little Wolf and his brother Big Nose were both good men in a fight—one as good as the other.[11]

By White Elk's account, Big Nose was killed during the battle. George Bent told a similar story, saying that Little Wolf let his younger brother, Swift Hawk, ride his white war pony and also gave him his scalp shirt, war bonnet, and lance. Both Swift Hawk and the horse were supposedly killed during the charge against the fort, and Little Wolf later buried his brother with all the accouterments he had worn during the battle.[12]

After the peace commission of 1867–68 had completed the Treaty of Medicine Lodge, Kansas, with the Southern bands, it moved on to Fort Laramie. General W. T. Sherman, whom President Ulysses S. Grant had removed from the commission prior to the Medicine Lodge council because of statements he had made against the Indians, was restored as head of the group. On May 10, 1868, a treaty with the Northern Cheyennes and Arapahoes was signed. Prominent among the Cheyennes who made their marks on the treaty document were Dull Knife, Little Wolf, and White Crow. By the treaty the Northern bands agreed to

> accept as a permanent home that portion of the reservation set apart for the Southern Cheyennes and Arapahoes by the Treaty of Medicine Lodge of October, 1867, or some portion of the reservation set apart for the Brulés and other bands of Sioux Indians by the treaty of April 29, 1868. Within one year of the date of the treaty, they will attach themselves permanently either to the agency provided near the mouth of Medicine Lodge Creek or to the agency about to be established on the Missouri River near Fort Randall, or to the Crow Agency near Otter Creek on the Yellowstone provided by the treaty of May 7, 1868, and it is hereby understood that one portion of said Indians may attach themselves to one of the aforementioned reservations and another portion to another of said reservations as each part or portion of said Indians (Cheyennes or Arapahoes) may elect.[13]

At the end of October, 1873, a delegation of Southern Cheyenne and Arapaho chiefs from the Darlington Agency, headed by Little Robe and Whirlwind and escorted by Agent John D. Miles, arrived in Washington, D.C. On November 3 they met with Commissioner of Indian Affairs E. P. Smith. Smith asked the Southern Cheyennes, who had recently conducted a frontier-alarming raid into Colorado against the Utes, for an end to the long-standing war with that tribe. Little Robe answered that the Cheyenne and Arapaho chiefs were for peace but that they would have to talk with their young men before making any binding agreements.[14]

A few days later, on November 8, another delegation of Cheyenne and Arapaho chiefs arrived. These were the Northern chiefs led by Dull Knife and Little Wolf and in the charge of General John E. Smith.[15] In a meeting with Commissioner E. P. Smith, the Northerners were told that by their treaty of 1868 they had ceded the country north of the Platte River to the whites and had agreed to go with the Southern bands. Dull Knife and Arapaho chief Plenty Bear told the commissioner that they had never given up their homelands in Nebraska and that they did not have the same understanding of the treaty that the whites had. Commissioner Smith answered that the Indians' "pretense of misunderstanding" would not do and that they would have to go south.[16]

Little Wolf and Dull Knife at Washington, D.C., in 1873, six years before their famous retreat from the Darlington Agency back to their northern homeland. The similarity between this photograph of Dull Knife and the photograph above from the National Archives is not clear, while Little Wolf appears much the same here and his his photograph above. *Courtesy of Smithsonian Institution, National Anthropological Archives, Neg. No. 270-a.*

A newspaper account, apparently giving the government's view, argued that the Northern Cheyennes and Arapahoes had agreed to go with the Crows, with the Sioux, or with the Southern bands. Since neither the Crows nor the Sioux wanted them, it was contended, they had to go south. Dull Knife and the other chiefs replied that they had come a long way to see the Great Father and that they were not satisfied to discuss the matter with subordinates. A meeting with President Ulysses S. Grant was arranged for the following day, November 14.

At eleven in the morning the chiefs arrived at the executive mansion and "formed a circle in the main lower hall, looking as stolid as tobacco signs."[17] Shortly they were escorted upstairs to the private office of the president, where they were introduced to the chief executive by Secretary of Interior Delano. Grant opened the conference by stating that the government desired to move the Indians south and that they would be much better provided for there. When Arapaho Little Bear gave a grunt in response, he was called upon to speak. He spoke briefly, saying that he had come a long way to see the Great Father and asking that the Arapahoes not be sent to the southern agency since they were happy where they were. Grant answered that by the treaty of 1868 the Indians had agreed to move south, but Little Chief contended that as he understood the treaty they were not to leave the northern agency for thirty-six years. Grant argued that the Indians would be better off in the south, where the climate was milder, the winters shorter, and the game more plentiful. Dull Knife then took the floor to say that when he signed the treaty he did not know he was required to go south at all. Grant's reply was that the interpreter must have been at fault, for he knew that General Sherman would never have done them any intentional injury. The conference ended with both Grant and the Indians holding their original views.

The firmness of Dull Knife and Little Wolf in refusing to be moved south won them and their people the reprieve of four years in which they continued to roam and hunt over the high grasslands of the north country. But in 1876 an event took place that reinforced the government's determination to force the move: Custer and the Seventh Cavalry were massacred on the Little Bighorn River by the Sioux and Northern Cheyennes. Neither Dull Knife nor Little Wolf was in on the fight; they were both on the Powder River at the time. But when they learned of Custer's defeat, they knew that more soldiers would come out. Dull Knife moved deeper into the Big Horn Mountains and went into camp near the head of Crazy Woman's Fork of the Powder River. Little Wolf and Wild Hog were with him.

Scouting forces under General Ranald S. Mackenzie discovered the Cheyenne village there, and early on the morning of November 26, 1876, mounted troops, supported by Pawnees, Shoshonis, and Bannocks, charged the encampment.[18] Despite heroic Cheyenne resistance, the village was swept under and captured, the Cheyennes were driven into the mountains, and all their goods and lodges were burned. Both Dull Knife and Little Wolf escaped into the mountains and eventually took refuge in the camps of the Sioux under Crazy Horse farther down the Powder River. Not all the Cheyennes were well received by the Sioux, however, and many of them spent a terrible winter without adequate provisions.

Later in November, Mackenzie sent out word asking the Cheyennes to surrender to him at Fort Robinson. Dull Knife's people agreed, and early in April, 1877, eighty lodges under Dull Knife and Standing Elk arrived at the Nebraska fort. The Indians were destitute to the extreme: they had lived through the winter months without lodges, possessing only old canvas and skins for shelters, and they had very few blankets and robes and no cooking utensils. Many of the 550 tribesmen had frozen limbs.[19]

The government was now determined to enforce the consolidation of the two branches of the Cheyennes. When the Northerners refused to go south voluntarily, rations were withheld from them until finally they consented to go on a trial basis. Under Dull Knife, Little Wolf, Crow, and Wild Hog, the Cheyennes made a difficult seventy-day trek southward to the Darlington Agency in Indian Territory, not far from present-day Oklahoma City. They arrived there under the blazing sun of August.

Almost immediately the Northerners were struck by an epidemic of fever and ague. Two-thirds of the nearly one thousand of them were stricken, their illness continuing through the winter. Contrary to Grant's promise that they would be better cared for in the south, the Indian Bureau offered only one physician to aid the five thousand or more Indians at Darlington, and he was not furnished with medical supplies until the spring of 1878. Forty-one of the Northern Cheyennes died that winter, and others suffered badly.[20]

In addition, the people from the north were, as Little Chief put it, "homesick and heartsick in every way."[21] The Southern Cheyennes called them fools and "Sioux." There were no buffalo to hunt, the woods were full of mosquitoes and ticks, and their rations consisted of ground cornmeal, which stirred up their bowels and made them sick. They could not forget the north country, where the climate was cooler, the air purer and healthier, and the water sweeter and better.[22] "We are sickly and dying here," they told Agent John D. Miles, "and no one will speak our names when we are gone.... We will go north at all hazards and if we die in battle, our names will be remembered and cherished by all our people."[23]

But Miles was adamant that the Cheyennes could not leave. He was told that three young Northern Cheyennes had stolen horses from the Southern tribes and gone north. The Southerners knew that it was the Northerners who were taking their horses because only the best ones were missing; white men would steal the whole herd. Miles ordered Little Wolf to send after the young men and bring them back. The chief answered that it would be impossible to do so. Miles ordered Captain Joseph Rendlebrock with two troops of cavalry to camp near the Northern Cheyennes and report their movements.[24]

After counciling on the matter, Little Wolf, Dull Knife, and the other headmen agreed: they would leave for the north with their people. On the night of September 9, 1878, they departed, some 353 of them. They left their campfires burning and tipi poles standing to fool the soldiers who were watching through the night from their camp. They moved rapidly for two days northwestward, reaching Turkey Springs north of the dry Cimarron River, where they were engaged by Rendlebrock and his two troops of Fourth Cavalry. Though Little Wolf had ordered that the Cheyennes not fight unless fired upon, evidence indicates that the young braves had killed three white men the day before Rendlebrock made contact on September 13.[25] The Cheyenne fighting force, drawn from the ninety-two men and sixty-nine boys with the fleeing band, engaged Rendlebrock's command in a standoff fight that resulted in three of the soldiers killed and three wounded and five of the Northern Cheyennes badly hurt.

The Indians continued on, crossing into Kansas, and on the eighteenth fought a brief skirmish with a small unit out of Camp Supply. Another minor encounter with soldiers occurred below the Arkansas River. There Little Wolf led a charge against the troops' wagons, drove off the guard, and captured some ammunition. Knowing there were too many soldiers to fight, Little Wolf moved his people all night, reaching the Arkansas River, where they met a party of buffalo hunters. The Cheyennes charged the party and captured it, but by Little Wolf's orders the hunters were released without harm. Eighteen slaughtered buffalo cows were taken for the Cheyennes to eat.[26]

After crossing the Arkansas River above Fort Dodge on September 23 or 24, another fight with soldiers occurred. Little Wolf made his men hold their fire until the soldiers were very close, making every shot count and routing the troops back to their wagon train. Next, along the Sappa and the Beaver rivers, the Cheyennes encountered civilians. A dispatch from Fort Wallace on October 4 reported:

> The Indians crossed the Kansas Pacific Railroad on Sunday morning (September 29), going north. When about 25 miles north of Buffalo Station they commenced killing settlers, and so far 17 dead bodies have been found along Sappa Creek. The Indians do not go out of their way at all to kill white people, but if they meet a man on horseback they kill him and take his horse. They are now 80 or 100 miles north of the Kansas Pacific Railroad, with troops pressing them pretty hard. They have killed no women nor children and have not thus far mutilated the bodies of their victims.[27]

Now Little Wolf and Dull Knife moved their people even faster, traveling at night and reaching the Frenchman's Fork of the Republican River in southern Nebraska. They saw no more troops and continued on without having to fight. They crossed the South Platte River above its juncture with the North Platte, finally camping near the mouth of White Clay Creek. Here Little Wolf and Dull Knife separated: Little Wolf headed on northward for the Powder River country while Dull Knife turned westward toward where he thought the Sioux agency of Red

Cloud was located. He did not know that it had been moved to the Dakotas at Pine Ridge.

On October 14 several men who were still living at the old Red Cloud Agency arrived at Fort Robinson to report that a party of Cheyennes had come to the agency and, before running off all the stock, had made inquiries as to the location of the new agency.[28] Cavalry units were immediately sent in search of the Indians, and on October 22 troops of the Third Cavalry scouting the sand hills about seventy miles southeast of Fort Robinson came upon some 150 Cheyennes under Dull Knife. The Cheyennes made ready to fight but, seeing that they were badly outnumbered, decided against it. Dull Knife surrendered and allowed his people to be taken to the soldiers' camp on Chadrone Creek, where the Indians' stock was taken away and they gave up some of their older guns. But when the Cheyennes learned that they were to be taken to Fort Robinson, they scattered over the prairie and began digging rifle pits with their hunting knives. It was necessary to call for artillery from Robinson before the Cheyennes could be rounded up and escorted in.[29]

Little Wolf, meanwhile, hid himself and his band in the Black Hills and wintered there. In the spring of 1879 he was on the Little Missouri River just northwest of the Black Hills. He was contacted there by Lieutenant W. P. Clark of Fort Keogh, who had been with Mackenzie when the Cheyenne village on the Powder River was captured in 1876. Clark requested that Little Wolf surrender peacefully.[30] The Cheyenne chief trusted Clark and agreed to surrender taking his people in to Fort Keogh, where they were received by General Nelson A. Miles. When Miles later invited the Cheyenne warriors to enlist as scouts for the army and fight against the Sioux, Little Wolf was at first reluctant but finally consented to do so.

Dull Knife and his band, however, were not so fortunate as Little Wolf. For several weeks things went well at Robinson. The Cheyennes were allowed their freedom as long as no one deserted. But one day it was discovered that Bull Hump was missing. He was caught and brought back, but now all the Cheyennes were placed in guarded buildings. The commanding officer, Captain Henry Wessels, insisted that the Indians agree to return south. He said that the Indian Bureau had ordered it in a letter.

Little Wolf with Lieutenant W. P. Clark in 1879 after the Cheyenne chief surrendered. It is difficult to accept this Indian as the same Little Wolf photographed with Dull Knife at Washington in 1873, though the identification is based on firm record in both cases. *Courtesy of Smithsonian Institution, National Anthropological Archives, Neg. No. 365-K.*

But Dull Knife would not agree. He told Wessels, "Great Grandfather sends death in that letter. You will have to kill us and take our bodies back down that trail. We will not go."[31]

Even when the soldiers stopped giving them rations, Dull Knife and the others refused to bend. Wessels now tried separating the women and children from the men so that he could deal with the men alone, but the Cheyennes still refused. Three of the men—Wild Hog, Crow, and Strong Left Hand—were talked into coming outside, and the soldiers grabbed Wild Hog to place him in irons.[32] Hog drew a concealed butcher knife and stabbed one of the soldiers. Strong Left Hand ran back to the barracks and told of the affair, and that night the young Cheyennes declared war and would no longer even talk with the whites. Wessels ordered that the Indians would have not only no food but also no water and no fuel to burn against the bitter cold. Still Dull Knife declared that the Cheyennes refused to go south, even if the alternative were starvation.

Finally on January 9, 1879, the Cheyennes decided that if they were to die they would rather do so on the open prairie they loved rather than shut up like dogs. That night shortly before dark, dressed in their best clothes and fully painted, Dull Knife and his son jumped through the windows of their barracks and ran for their lives. The other Cheyennes followed. The post alarm was quickly sounded, and the soldiers poured out of their quarters in their white underwear, firing at the fleeing Indians. Many of the Cheyennes were killed, and many recaptured. Dull Knife and his family hid among the rocks in the hills for nearly ten days, almost starving and freezing to death before finally reaching the Pine Ridge Agency. The determination of the Northern Cheyennes never again to leave their homeland is illustrated in an account by a newspaper correspondent:

> One Indian, who was attended by his wife, and who was being closely pursued by some soldiers prior to reaching the cave, was appealed to by his wife to surrender, and thus save both of their lives. Seeing that escape was impossible he plunged his knife into the breast of his wife exclaiming, "You shall not be taken back to the South," and then shot himself through the heart. The woman survived the blow, and now resides at the Red Cloud Agency. In the cave, a mother made a similar unsuccessful attempt on the life of her daughter. Old Dull Knife, father of the young chief, who was supposed to have been killed in the cave, managed to elude the

troops on the night of the outbreak, and is now living at Pine Ridge.[33]

Following the Camp Robinson affair in 1879, Colonel George A. Woodward, a former commander of Fort Fetterman who had met Dull Knife and Little Wolf when the Northern Cheyennes had visited his fort in the spring of 1871, summed up his impressions of these two great chiefs:

> Of the three head-men of the Cheyennes, Dull Knife was, I think, greatly the superior. Tall and lithe in form, he had the face of a statesman or church dignitary of the grave and aesthetic type. His manner of speech was earnest and dignified, and his whole bearing was that of a leader with the cares of state. Little Wolf had a less imposing presence, but looked more the soldier than the statesman.[34]

Dull Knife died in the early 1880's and was buried on the Rosebud River. Little Wolf lived out his life on the Tongue River Indian Reservation in Montana. During the winter of 1880, Little Wolf killed Starving Elk in a drunken quarrel over the attention the latter was paying to Wolf's daughter. Because he had broken his faith as a chief by committing murder, Little Wolf went into voluntary exile along the Rosebud River away from his people. There he grew blind and helpless before dying in 1904.[35]

LITTLE CHIEF

Even as Little Wolf and Dull Knife were fighting their way north in September, 1878, another band of Northern Cheyennes was being moved southward from Fort Abraham Lincoln in Dakota Territory to Darlington Agency. Headed by Little Chief,[35] they were being escorted by four companies of Fourth Cavalry and guided by Ben Clark, Custer's former scout who had a Cheyenne wife in Indian Territory. At Sidney, Nebraska, where news of Dull Knife and Little Wolf reached the expedition, Little Chief's people were disarmed for fear they would join the other Northerners. But Little Chief's band made no trouble, not even killing a cow or pig that belonged to a white settler to eat on the way. They reached Darlington in early December.

Little Chief's band of Northern Cheyennes had surrendered at
Red Cloud Agency in March, 1877, following a series of defeats
at the hands of United States troops. After their surrender, some
of the Cheyennes had volunteered as scouts to help General
Nelson A. Miles find and fight the Minniconjou Sioux under
Chief Lame Deer in May, 1877. It had been Cheyennes, in fact,
who had killed Chief Lame Deer in the attack. Later, in September, some thirty Cheyenne scouts had served with Miles's
forces against Chief Joseph's Nez Percés, who were retreating
up the Yellowstone River.[36] Miles promised Little Chief and his
people that if they came south and did not like it, they would be
allowed to return. The government knew the valuable services
they had rendered, the officer said.[37]

Little Chief's band soon found that they could endure the
warm climate of Indian Territory no better than their fellow
Northerners under Little Wolf and Dull Knife. Many became ill,
including Little Chief's grown son, who died not long after their
arrival at Darlington. And, unlike the Northerners under Standing Elk who had relatives among the Southern Cheyennes, Little
Chief's band was not compatible with the Southerners.[38]

Little Chief strongly expressed his dissatisfaction with being
located at Darlington and insisted that he and his people should
be allowed to return north. In May, 1879, he and five other
Cheyenne leaders traveled to Washington, where they presented their grievances to government officials. They had caused
no trouble coming south, he said, nor would he and his people
leave without government approval; but he had been promised
that they could return, and they wanted to do so. Officials in
Washington led Little Chief to believe that he would be given
approval to return north, and he went home fully expecting to
be leaving Indian Territory soon. But the order did not come.

Then in August, 1879, a congressional committee visited Fort
Reno and interviewed Little Chief at length. Little Chief told
them that after his surrender in the north he had been taken to
Chicago for a talk with General Sheridan, who had promised
him that if they came south their horses and guns would not be
taken from them. But when they reached Darlington, white officials went ahead and confiscated the Indians' firearms and
horses. In fact, their horses were taken to Camp Supply and sold
by the Quartermaster Department, and the Indians were given

Little Chief, Northern Cheyenne leader. "Little Chief is . . . tall, and of commanding appearance, and Indian though he be he has more brain power than some of the white milksops the newspapers advertize as great statesmen."—*Caldwell Commercial. Courtesy of Smithsonian Institution.*

only eleven dollars apiece for the horses, regardless of the kind. "I think when they sold them they just gave us back whatever they saw fit," Little Chief told the senators.[39]

He said, also, that he refused to allow the children of his band to be sent to school because "I love my children and do not want to see them made slaves of."[40] He complained strongly that the rations for his band were insufficient. The sugar was never over a handful, and they got only a peck of flour a week for ten families. The yellow cornmeal which the government provided the Indians made them sick. Only one beef per week was issued to thirty or thirty-five Indians, and that was generally gone in two or three days. No clothing had been issued to them. He and his people wished to return to "the land God gave us," Little Chief said. "We never get sick there."[41] He also pointed out that it did not make his people feel good to hang about an agency and have to beg a white man for something to eat when they got hungry.

Despite his strong resentment against the government for the bad treatment of his people, Little Chief was adamantly opposed to his band's returning north without approval. In the fall of 1880 some of his young men attempted to incite the other Cheyennes to follow them north. Little Chief took up his gun and rode about the camps instructing his people to remain at Darlington and threatening to kill anyone who attempted to leave.[42]

Little Chief had begun to understand something of the politics of the whites. He had learned that every four years the white people's government changed to some extent, and he hoped for a change in policy concerning his returning north. In August, 1881, he made a second trip to Washington, and this time he won more than empty promises. The commissioner of Indian Affairs approved the return of Little Chief's band to Pine Ridge Reservation in the north. Though Pine Ridge was not the Cheyenne home on the Tongue River, the decision much pleased Little Chief, and on October 6, 1881, he and his people began their march northward. They reached Pine Ridge in December, 1881, after three years in the south.[43]

Pine Ridge was to be their home for the next ten years, though Little Chief continued to agitate to be returned to Fort Keogh, at the mouth of the Tongue River. He also continued his pleas for better food and treatment. Agent V. T. McGillycuddy, unappreciative of Little Chief's influence in keeping his band on

the peace road, considered the Cheyenne leader as troub-
lemaker.[44] Finally in 1891, largely because Little Chief and his
band had done as the government asked in giving up the Sun
Dance ceremony and had not participated the Ghost Dance of
1890, they were permitted to move to the Tongue River Reservation in eastern Montana. At long last Little Chief had led his
people back to the land God gave them.[45]

Delegation of chiefs at Washington, D.C., in 1871. *Standing, left to
right:* interpreter Edmond Guerrier, who served as guide for Custer
on his first campaign against the Indians; Kaw agent Mahlon Stubbs;
long-time Cheyenne interpreter and frontiersman John Simpson Smith;
and Philip McCusker, Comanche interpreter who was at Fort Cobb
when the Washita fight occurred. *Seated, left to right:* Arapaho chief Little
Raven, Cheyenne chiefs Bird Chief and Little Robe, and Wichita chief
Buffalo Goad. *Courtesy of Smithsonian Institution, Bureau of America,
Ethnology Collection.*

10

The Reservation Chiefs

Little Robe, Stone Calf, Minimic

*We are at peace and desire to go that road, and we
want you to help us get back our women and children
that were taken from us last fall.*

Minimic

In the year 1869 and following, the Southern Cheyennes were a
starved, desperate people. They had been driven first from their
homes in Colorado and then from the prairies of western Kansas. Following the Washita massacre they were constant prey to
the military forces of the whites, who demanded their submis-
sion to reservation life. Life on a reservation, the Cheyennes
soon learned, meant not only an end to their freedom to roam at
will and hunt on the open plains but also a precarious depen-
dence upon the whites for food and other supplies.

They were forced to watch as white buffalo hunters slaughtered the buffalo by the thousands, to accept virtually without
defense the encroachment of white horse thieves and whisky
peddlers onto their lands, and to submit their way of life to
the wishes and dictates of bureaucratic government officials.
They were asked to give up the life of a warrior and to take up
that of a farmer or rancher, contrary to their established culture.
They were pressured to send their children to the schools of the
whites, some of them in far off lands, where they would be
taught to be white men and not Indians.

During the decade from 1869 to 1879 the fighting tradition
and spirit of the Cheyenne war societies were by no means
entirely submissive to white dominance. There would still be
acts of defiance by the hot-blooded Cheyenne warriors and
warriors-to-be. But it was within the wisdom of the Cheyenne
peace chiefs to understand that the weight of white civilization
was overwhelming and inevitable, and it was through their lead-

143

ership that reconciliation was ultimately brought about. Three Cheyenne chiefs, perhaps more than others during this period, stood out as the peace leaders who brought their people to final, unhappy acceptance of reservation life and, to some extent, the white man's road. They were Little Robe, Stone Calf, and Minimic.

LITTLE ROBE

Following the death of Black Kettle at the Washita River the leading peace chief of the Southern Cheyennes was Little Robe.[1] A gentle-natured man, he nonetheless bore numerous scars about his body from the many battles of his warrior days. Hubert Collins, as a boy became friends with the Cheyenne leader during the winter of 1883–84 at Red Fork Ranch on the Chisholm Cattle Trail, and he later recalled the stories that Little Robe told of his people in the mellow voice and sign language of the Indian. "One could not associate with the man," Collins wrote, "and not recognize the spirit and friend of his people."[2]

Little Robe had gained prominence as a warrior in Cheyenne battles with the Pawnees, Utes, and other enemy tribes as early as 1853. In the spring of that year, following the death of Alights-on-the-Cloud and other important men in the big fight with the Pawnees in 1852, Little Robe carried the Cheyenne pipe of mourning about to the various Cheyenne camps on the South Platte River and Beaver Creek.[3]

Though he was not a signer of the Treaty of Fort Wise in 1861, Little Robe had become a chief by 1863 when Elbridge Gerry visited the Cheyenne camps for John Evans, governor of Colorado Territory. The chiefs, their tribes decimated by smallpox, refused to enter into a pact with Evans.[4] In 1864, however, Little Robe was one of those casting their lot with Black Kettle's peace faction, taking his family, lodge, and horses to Sand Creek. Though he himself escaped from the early morning avalanche of soldiers that fell upon the village, his family was wiped out with the exception of one son.[5] George Bent later wrote of saying good-bye to Little Robe and Black Kettle following the Sand Creek attack as he left to go north and join the Cheyenne and Arapaho soldier societies in their war against the whites. Little Robe, who had lost his tipi, ponies, and virtually all of his personal property, went south of the Arkansas River with Black Kettle.[6]

Little Robe remained with the peace faction after the Sand Creek disaster and was present at the Treaty of the Little Arkansas in 1865. When Agent Edward W. Wynkoop visited the Cheyennes on Bluff Creek in southern Kansas in February, 1866, Little Robe was with the mixed blood Edmond Guerrier on the Solomon River, trying to bring in the Dog Soldiers and others for peace talks. He was successful in bringing them in; but the end result was that the powerful Cheyenne war societies forced both Little Robe and Black Kettle to withdraw their assent to the amendments Congress had made to the Little Arkansas treaty.[7]

Little Robe had been among the chiefs interviewed by General Winfield Scott Hancock on the Pawnee Fork in April, 1867. He also played an important role at the Medicine Lodge treaty council, acting as an intermediary between the peace commissioners and the main Cheyenne encampment, which was then much under the dominance of the Dog Soldiers. It was Little Robe who reported that the tardy Cheyennes were making their great medicine lodge and conducting their ceremony of renewal of the Medicine Arrows and that they would thus be delayed in attending the council. His signature appears on the Medicine Lodge treaty.[8]

The Cheyenne peace chief was also on the Washita River when Custer attacked in November, 1868. Little Robe had been with Black Kettle when, just before the massacre, they had visited Fort Cobb to talk with General William M. Hazen, and his encampment was just downstream from Black Kettle's camp. On December 31, 1868, Little Robe and twenty other leaders of the Cheyennes and Arapahoes arrived at Fort Cobb. They came by foot, wrapped in their blankets against the cold, to say that their people, still mourning the loss of relatives and friends at the Washita, were starving. There were no buffalo, and they had eaten even their last camp dog. The chiefs had walked to Fort Cobb because their horses were too weak to be ridden.[9]

The hot-tempered, rough-talking Sheridan threatened to make war on the Cheyennes winter and summer until they were wiped out if they did not come in to their reservation. He told

Little Robe that if the tribes did not make a "complete" peace, the soldiers would go back to fighting. "It is for you to say what we have to do," Little Robe said, so submissively that the blustering Sheridan was taken aback.[10]

True to his word, Little Robe, along with Minimic, brought his band in to the new reservation at Camp Supply, where the new agent, Quaker Brinton Darlington, had established his agency temporarily. Little Robe was a great help to Darlington, going out to Cheyenne camps on Beaver and Wolf creeks to persuade absentee bands to come in.

In the spring of 1871, a delegation of Indian chiefs, including Little Robe and Stone Calf, was escorted to Washington, D.C., and on a tour of several eastern cities—Philadelphia, New York City, Boston, and others—before returning by train via Chicago. At Washington Little Robe and the others had an interview with President Ulysses S. Grant and later visited the Treasury Department, where they encountered their first elevators. In New York they were taken to visit the Central Park zoo and saw a wondrous variety of strange animals. They were equally astounded at the number of large ships in the harbor and dismayed when they learned the vessels carried loads of new immigrants. In New England they visited the campus of Harvard University, which Little Robe conceded might be a good place to educate his son.[11]

In his interview with Little Robe, President Grant had promised that the Indians on the plains would be given protection by the army. But it proved to be an empty and futile promise, for white horse thieves from Indian Territory and southern Kansas were regularly raiding Cheyenne horse herds. When Little Robe's son Sitting Medicine and two other braves followed one gang and located their hideout on the Cimarron, a gunfight ensued. Sitting Medicine was severely wounded.[12]

During 1873 government surveyors came into Indian Territory. The Cheyennes, knowing full well that the surveyors preceded further white intrusion, wrecked a camp in March of that year. Little Robe went against tribal practice and identified Foolish Bear as the culprit. Struggling to keep his young men from making trouble, Little Robe brought his band in to Camp Supply in September, 1873, along with the bands of Stone Calf, Whirlwind, White Shield, Pawnee, and White Horse. However,

Little Robe and White Horse, Southern Cheyenne chiefs, at Washington, D.C., in 1873. *Courtesy of Smithsonian Institution, National Anthropological Archives, Neg. No. 349.*

Little Robe and Stone Calf, the prime leaders of the Cheyenne peace faction, were angry with the government over its failure to return stolen Cheyenne horses from Kansas.[13]

In November, 1873, Little Robe accompanied Stone Calf, Whirlwind, White Horse, White Shield, Pawnee, and an Arapaho group to Washington, D.C., where they signed articles of agreement with the government redefining their reservation area as established by the Treaty of Medicine Lodge. The fact that Stone Calf was the first to sign and Little Robe second indicates that the former had now ascended to a position in the tribe more prominent than that of Little Robe.[14]

By now Little Robe had grown weary of the fine words that flowed in meetings with the Great Father. When it came his turn to speak, he stood up before Grant and said, "I have come a good ways to see the Great Father. I now see him. That is all I have to say."[15] Grant laughed and commented to an aide that after this he might lose his reputation as a terse speaker.

During 1874 bloody war returned to the plains. On July 4, 1874, wagon freighter Pat Hennessey and three companions were massacred by a Cheyenne war party on the Chisholm Trail in Indian Territory. Hennessey was tied to a wagon wheel and burned to death. On August 26, O. F. Short and five members of his surveying crew were murdered near Lone Tree, forty miles south and twenty west of Dodge, by a war party under Medicine Water. Then on September 11, Medicine Water attacked a party of immigrants near the Kansas-Colorado border, killing John Germain (or German) his wife, and older daughter and taking the four younger Germain girls captive.[16]

The soldier societies now had the upper hand in tribal councils, and the peace leaders were intimidated to such a point that they were ordered not to leave their villages. When Little Robe attempted to leave the main camps and go to Darlington, his horses were shot and killed. Despite this, he eventually joined White Shield, Pawnee, and Whirlwind at the agency in August, 1874, remaining aloof from the war that lasted into 1875.[17]

Along with Stone Calf and White Shield, Little Robe took up permanent residence on the reservation near Cantonment, halfway between Fort Reno and Camp Supply on the North Canadian River. Here he joined in opposing Agent John D. Miles's grass-lease program in an effort to keep white cattlemen and

Whirlwind and Pawnee, Southern Cheyenne chiefs, at Washington, D.C., 1873. *Courtesy of Smithsonian Institution, Bureau of American Ethnology Collection, Neg. No. 348.*

their herds off the Cheyenne lands. He refused to send children from his band to white schools and to join in a program whereby the Cheyennes and Arapahoes would freight their own goods from Kansas. Still, Little Robe was not entirely hostile to white ways, as is evident from the occasional shopping trips he made to Wichita.[18] But as the decade of the 1880's came, the aging Little Robe had begun to fall in the shadows of other chiefs, particularly Stone Calf, who had become the titular leader of the Cantonment Cheyennes and who stood against the more progressive chiefs at Darlington on issues such as grass leasing and schooling for their children.

STONE CALF

Stone Calf[19] was, perhaps, the dominant chief of the Southern Cheyennes during the early reservation period following the last Cheyenne outbreak of 1874, being even more influencial than Little Robe. Like most of the other Cheyenne chiefs, he had been a renowned warrior in his younger days. When General Sheridan had arrived on the Kansas frontier in the fall of 1868 to talk with the Cheyennes at Fort Larned, Agent Wynkoop had asked permission to issue arms and ammunition to the Cheyennes as had been promised by the Treaty of Medicine Lodge. "Yes, give them arms," Sheridan had snapped sarcastically, "and if they go to war the soldiers can kill them like men." Whereupon Stone Calf had answered, "Let your soldiers grow long hair, so that we can have some honor in killing them." Sheridan had managed a smile, saying that he would be afraid that his soldiers would get lousy.[20]

Stone Calf had played no noticeable role at the Medicine Lodge council, but following the Washita affair he came to prominence as a leading chief of the Cheyennes. He was the only chief present in April, 1870, when the Quaker Indian agents arrived in Indian Territory and conducted a council with the various tribes on the North Fork of the Canadian River, near what was later the site of the Darlington Agency.[21]

Stone Calf made a brief speech at that time in which he indicated his willingness to try the white man's peace road. "The old father, our agent [Darlington], sent for me to come down here. I

White Shield, Southern Cheyenne chief, photographed before 1877. *Courtesy of Smithsonian Institution, National Anthropological Archives, Neg. No. 322.*

came down expecting to see many of my friends, and I am glad to see them. I am very glad to shake hands with all here. My people are far away, and I am by myself. I am glad the agent talks of farming, and I would like to settle down and live here. I am very glad to see all my friends."[22]

Accordingly, it was Stone Calf, with thirteen Cheyenne lodges and with George Bent and John Simpson Smith and their families, who first accompanied Agent Darlington to the site of the new agency in May, 1870. The willingness of Stone Calf to go this far east to a reservation was of much benefit to Darlington and helped to lure other bands there. When Quaker Indian official William Nicholson visited the agency in November, 1870, he found not only Stone Calf but Little Robe, Minimic, Big Jake, Grey Beard, Heap of Birds, Big Horse, Red Moon, Whirlwind, and a number of other important Cheyenne headmen as well.[23]

When the Kiowas attempted to lure the Cheyenne warriors off on raids into Texas, it was Stone Calf and Little Robe who did the most in restraining the young Cheyennes. Because of their importance and peace proclivities, Stone Calf and Little Robe were chosen to visit Washington, D.C., in 1871. Stone Calf took his wife with him. During the trip Stone Calf was a good spokesman for his people. In Washington he reminded officials of their promise to render agricultural aid. "We haven't an ax," he told them, "we haven't an acre of corn growing today in our great country that the Government has said they would reserve for us."[24]

Later he voiced his concern on other matters. The railroads, he said, were of no use to the Cheyennes. The men who built the railroads and the "evil ones who remained behind" once the tracks were laid inevitably brought trouble with them. To the Cheyennes, surveyors were the first step by the whites in taking their lands. When a government surveying party working in Indian Territory in December of 1872 was given emphatic warning to get out and stay out, it was not an idle threat.

There were other serious problems besetting the Cheyennes. Nefarious white traders working back and forth across the Kansas–Indian Territory line were keeping a heavy flow of whisky coming to the Indian tribes. Not only did it cause debauchery and trouble among the Cheyenne warriors, but when

Stone Calf and wife, at Washington, D.C., in 1873. *Courtesy of Smithsonian Institution, Bureau of American Ethnology Collection, Neg. no. 283.*

the traders raised their prices it placed a severe hardship on the Cheyenne women, who already worked industriously from morning until night preparing buffalo robes. Finally the Indian women rebelled by slowing down their efforts.[25]

When Agent John D. Miles attempted to gain some control by confiscating the goods of an old Delaware Indian bringing whisky, guns, and ammunition into Indian Territory, Stone Calf charged that the agent had broken the word given in Washington that he could get more guns and ammunition for his people. It was a serious matter to the Cheyennes, who argued that they needed weapons and bullets in order to hunt game to feed themselves.

Gangs of white horse thieves who raided the Cheyenne herds posed another grave problem. Hardly anything was more precious to a native of the plains than his horse: it was not only transportation and a vehicle of mobility in war but also the measure of wealth for a man. Although all of the Plains Indians were notorious intertribal horse stealers, it was especially hard on the Indians to have white men stealing their horses. While the troops could not or would not prevent white men from stealing the Cheyenne horses, they could and would interfere if the Cheyennes stole horses from the whites. Horse theft was a very sore issue with Stone Calf and Little Robe, and it led to serious quarrels with Agent Miles.

Despite the visit to Washington in November, 1873, by Stone Calf, Little Robe, and other Cheyenne chiefs, the peace on the reservation began to break apart. The Cheyenne warriors were becoming more and more discontent and restless. Stone Calf, Little Robe, and the other peace chiefs began losing their control over the young men of the warrior societies. In April, 1873, four men of the Barrett surveying party were massacred on the Cimarron by Cheyenne warriors.[26] During 1874 horses belonging to the Darlington Agency were stolen, buffalo hunters were attacked on the plains, three settlers were killed and scalped near Medicine Lodge, Kansas, and a small military party was attacked north of Camp Supply.[27]

Then on June 27, 1874, the Comanches, Kiowas, Arapahoes, and Cheyennes launched a united attack on the buffalo hunters' camp at Adobe Walls. Though Stone Calf took no part in the battle himself, his son was killed during the fight.[28] It is not clear what role Stone Calf played in the fall of 1874 as United States troops searched the rough canyon-gashed country of the Texas Panhandle in an attempt to capture or destroy the Cheyenne hostiles under Grey Beard. Virtually all of the Cheyenne bands were out from the reservation, and it was impossible to separate the peace-minded from the war-minded. Unlike Little Robe and a few of the others who escaped the fierce domination of the Dog Soldiers, Stone Calf remained with the hostiles. In November he sent word to the agency that he wished to surrender, but he and his band failed to show up when expected.

A surrender was arranged in February, 1875. Though Stone Calf's men had not committed the attack on the Germain family of immigrants, his band had become involved when the two older girls were brought to his camp. Now Stone Calf attempted to use the girls to bargain with during his surrender; but when this tactic was unsuccessful, he escorted an ambulance back to his camp to pick up the girls.[29] Stone Calf was not held responsible for the crimes of capture and rape committed against the Germain girls and was not among those arrested and sent to the Fort Marion, Florida, prison.

Following his surrender, Stone Calf joined Little Robe and White Shield in settling his band near the army's Cantonment post. Though still a leading peace advocate, he was the dominant figure in opposition to Miles's grass-lease plan for the Cheyennes. Agent Miles, seeking to improve the financial situation of the Cheyennes by leasing reservation lands to white cattlemen, had made arrangements with eight leasees, dividing into eight sections the new three-million-acre-plus reservation, which had been established by the 1873 agreement.

Cantonment, in the district assigned to the firm of Lee and Reynolds, was located on the branch of the Chisholm Trail that cut northwestward along the North Canadian River toward Dodge City. In addition to the trail herds that passed across Cheyenne lands, the intrusion of grazier herds caused problems. Stone Calf complained bitterly to Miles that this was "hard on him and there was no grass for his ponies."[30] The Indians found that their livestock was constantly getting lost among the huge cattle herds, but many simply did not like having the cattlemen and cowboys on their land.

Stone Calf, Little Robe, and White Shield refused to take part in the grass leasing, even to the point of not accepting their portion of lease payments. It was partially their adamant opposition that eventually caused Miles, who had staked his job on the grass-lease plan, to resign in the spring of 1884. The new agent, D. B. Dyer, no sooner arrived at Darlington than an incident near Cantonment caused serious agitation of the problem. A Texas drover named Horton ran his horse herd over the garden patch of a Cheyenne named Running Buffalo. A shooting culminated in the murder of Running Buffalo.[31]

This incident and continued opposition by Stone Calf and the other Cantonment Cheyennes stirred up considerable fuss over the grass-lease program, until in July, 1885, President Grover Cleveland dispatched Generals Phil Sheridan and Nelson Miles to Indian Territory to investigate. Sheridan interviewed Stone Calf at Darlington and heard the chief vehemently deny Agent Dyer's charges that the Cantonment Cheyennes were seeking trouble with the whites. Stone Calf charged that George Bent, a mixed-blood chief of the Cheyennes, had told the Cheyennes that their annuities would be withheld if they did not sign the lease agreement.[32]

Sheridan sided with Stone Calf and Little Robe against Agent Dyer. On his recommendation the grass-lease program on Cheyenne land was cancelled by executive order, and Dyer was removed as agent. When the new agent, Captain J. M. Lee, arrived and called a meeting of the Cheyenne leaders, it was Stone Calf who dominated, calling for a greater issue of rations to his people and demanding that a school be built at Cantonment for his children. He also insisted that whites be stopped from killing game on his land and cutting down trees to make fences in the Cherokee Strip.[33]

Stone Calf died in November, 1885, near Cantonment. Little Robe led the burial procession which carried the Cheyenne chief to his resting place on the banks of the Washita River. The *Cheyenne Transporter,* the Darlington newspaper which had been begun as an Indian sheet but which had become decidedly pro-cattleman, unsympathetically opined that Stone Calf had been "a very bad man, but he is now a good one. . . . Before his death he drew a plow from Agent Dyer and promised he would walk in the white man's path and be a good Indian. The latter vow he kept."[34]

All too often the whites defined a "good chief" as one who let the whites have their way in all things. Stone Calf had not done that. Instead he fought resolutely for the rights of his people, while remaining essentially peaceful.

MINIMIC, OR EAGLE'S HEAD

Cheyenne histories have largely overlooked the importance of Minimic[35] as a peace chief, mentioning him only occasionally. But the records give testimony to his strength of character and leadership in the cause of peace, particularly as the principal Cheyenne among the Saint Augustine, Florida, prisoners from 1875 to 1878.

Minimic, who became better known by his Indian name than by the English translation "Eagle's Head," first came to notice in 1864. When Black Kettle wrote his peace letter in August of that year, before the Sand Creek Massacre, and dispatched One Eye and his wife to take it in to Fort Lyon, a Cheyenne brave stepped forward. Although One Eye's daughter was married to a white man who lived near Fort Lyon, the soldiers had orders to shoot first and ask questions later whenever Indians were met. Minimic insisted that he would not let them go alone.[36] It was clearly an act of courage for Minimic to join One Eye in this effort to bring peace to the plains. After the three were taken and placed in the Fort Lyon guardhouse, Minimic willingly agreed to be a hostage for Major Wynkoop and his troops when they rode deep into the Indian country of western Kansas to meet with Black Kettle and the other Cheyenne and Arapaho chiefs.[37]

During the dark days following Sand Creek, when the Dog Soldiers were striking the wagon roads and frontier settlements throughout Kansas, Nebraska, and Colorado, Minimic went with Black Kettle and his peace faction to the country south of the Arkansas River, refusing to take part in the Dog Soldier war of retribution. He was present at the signing of the Treaty of the Little Arkansas in August, 1865, and later signed the revised pact along with Black Kettle, Little Robe, and others.[38]

Minimic was also present at the Medicine Lodge treaty council in 1867, helping to keep the peace between the Dog Soldiers and Black Kettle, whom the war chiefs were threatening. The fact that the Dog Soldiers were dominant at Medicine Lodge perhaps explains why Minimic did not sign the treaty. On the night of October 20 at Medicine Lodge, according to reporter Henry M. Stanley, the commissioners' camp was visited by Black Kettle, Little Robe, Grey Beard, and Minimic. The chiefs enjoyed a hearty meal and, after "a preliminary smoke from the inevitable calumet," talked with the commissioners. They assured the commission that the tardy Cheyennes would come in just as soon as they were finished with their Medicine Arrow ceremony.[39]

Following Custer's massacre of the Cheyennes on the Washita River, Minimic found himself just as much a refugee on the prairies as the hostiles among the Cheyennes. He was among the chiefs who appeared at Fort Cobb on December 31, 1868, to sue for peace with General Sheridan. He was also one of the first to persuade his people to take the chance of surrendering to the whites, bringing his band to Fort Sill on April 7, 1869.[40]

Later the Cheyenne chief moved his village to the new reservation at Camp Supply. He was there on April 22, 1870, as the leading spokesman for the Cheyennes in a conference with the new Quaker Indian Superintendent Enock Hoag. Minimic told Hoag that the Cheyennes appreciated the government's offer to build them new homes on the North Canadian River. But, he said, there were still plenty of buffalo, and they could still kill the animals and build their own hide houses for a while longer. "We, the Cheyennes," Minimic insisted, "have never claimed this land. We once lived further north. We did not come here from choice, but we were compelled to come; and if it is best for us to live further down [further to the east where Darlington Agency was established the following year], we will do so, and be at peace."[41]

Minimic said they had promised General Sheridan they would be at peace and they would. But the Cheyennes hoped they would be indulged a while longer to live by hunting and by making robes to exchange for the trade goods they needed. They had asked for ammunition to hunt the deer and turkey that were so abundant in the region, but Colonel Anderson D. Nelson at Camp Supply had refused. They did not want to go to war, Minimic promised, and were willing to go to work and raise corn

Minimic, or Eagle's Head, photographed by William S. Soule at Fort Sill, ca. 1870. "During their captivity, Minimic, above all others, exerted the greatest influence for good over the others, and all matters of dispute arising were referred to him for final settlement."—*Wichita Eagle.* *Courtesy of Smithsonian Institution.*

159

on their land. "We are at peace," he told Hoag, "and desire to go that road, and we want you to help us get back our women and children that were taken from us last fall."[42]

During the summer of 1873, the Cheyennes under Little Robe, Minimic, Stone Calf, and White Horse remained under the custody of the military at Camp Supply. As hostilities developed during 1873 and 1874, it became more and more difficult for the chiefs to restrain their young men. The Cheyennes were seriously disturbed by the intense slaughter of buffalo on the prairies by white buffalo hunters. According to George Bent, even Minimic fought as a warrior in the long-range duel with Billy Dixon and the buffalo hunters at Adobe Walls on June 27, 1874.[43]

There was no doubt that Minimic represented the peace faction of the Cheyennes. But when the government decided to imprison the most hostile of the Cheyennes and those who were accused of crimes, Minimic became a hapless victim of circumstance. Men of the tribe were rounded up at Darlington Agency and placed in a line. Cheyenne interpreter Romero was ordered by Lieutenant Colonel Thomas Neill to pick out the worst offenders. Romero, who later said he was drunk at the time, began pointing out certain of the Indians, but it was late in the evening and darkness began closing in before the chore was completed. Finally Neill ordered his men to "cut off eighteen from the right of the line." Minimic was among this group, and on the afternoon of April 6, 1875, he was lined up with the others for the "ironing" process—that is, being placed in leg irons.[44]

When the first Cheyenne was brought forward to be shackled, the warrior made a break for freedom and was shot and killed by the guard. Then all the Cheyennes bolted for the nearby sand hills, where they had weapons and ammunition stowed, and a general fight resulted. Many of the Cheyennes were recaptured, and in early May thirty-one men and one woman were taken in irons and under the guard of a company of cavalry to Fort Sill. Minimic, Grey Beard, and Heap of Birds were among them. After being held for a time at Sill, the Cheyennes were entrained for Fort Marion at Saint Augustine, Florida. They enjoyed no trial, or even a hearing, before imprisonment.[45]

Between Red Oak and Lake City, Florida, Grey Beard jumped from the train, which was traveling at twenty-five miles per hour.

The train was stopped, and the guard hunted the bushes for Grey Beard. The chief was flushed and shot as he ran to escape. He died two hours later.[46]

During the three-year incarceration of the Cheyennes at Fort Marion, Minimic, above all others, was the peacemaker and mediator, exerting his influence for good relations whenever disputes arose. All matters were referred to him for final settlement.[47] The Cheyennes were treated as military prisoners and had to practice military drills regularly.

When they were finally released and returned to Indian Territory in April, 1878, the Cheyennes were brought by military escort to Wichita and turned over to Agent Miles. Wichita Mayor William Greiffenstein, who had once been a trader among the Cheyennes, made a "welcome back" speech to the Indians at the Occidental Hotel. Minimic and the others hugged and shook little "Dutch Bill" with such enthusiasm that citizens feared for him.

Minimic, wearing the uniform of a United States soldier, visited the offices of the Wichita *Eagle* with Greiffenstein. The editor described the chief as a "fine looking man physically, with an intelligent and kind face." Now speaking English quite well, Minimic said without bitterness that he had never quite understood why he had been taken away from the rolling prairies of the buffalo to the barren beach sands of Florida. Though some of his young men had been into mischief, he himself "had violated no treaty."[48]

Minimic returned to the Darlington Agency, where the government now forced the Northern Cheyennes to live. When Dull Knife and Little Wolf made their famous retreat across Kansas to their old haunts in the north, Minimic wrote a letter to an army officer, saying, "Don't give yourself any trouble about the 'Sioux-Cheyenne' who ran away; they loved the country up north, and could not be persuaded to remain here."[49] Minimic remained at Darlington until he died on May 16, 1881.

These Cheyenne men and others stood tall, their blankets wrapped about them and their bronze faces unblinking, as they watched the world they knew and loved disappear forever. The open prairies, the free-flowing streams, the great herds of buffalo that provided them a hunter's livelihood, their existence as a free people all vanished before their eyes within the span of a single lifetime. The Cheyenne Nation left its imprint cut deeply across the American West. But perhaps its greatest achievement was the leaders it produced, warriors turned peacemakers, the Cheyenne chiefs.

Notes

CHAPTER I

1. George A. Dorsey, *The Cheyenne,* Field Columbia Museum Publication 99, Anthology Series, Vol. 9, No. 1 (Chicago: March, 1905), pp. 12–15; John Stands In Timber and Margot Liberty, *Cheyenne Memories* (New Haven: Yale University Press, 1967), pp. 42–52; George Bird Grinnell, *The Cheyenne Indians, Their History and Ways of Life* (New Haven: Yale University Press, 1923), Vol. 1 of 2, pp. 336–344.

2. Garrard thought the Cheyennes had gotten this crossing notion from the Catholic French whom they met on the Upper Mississippi during the seventeenth century. Lewis H. Garrard, *Wah-to-Yah and the Taos Trail* (Norman: University of Oklahoma Press, 1955), p. 69.

3. Stands In Timber and Liberty, *Cheyenne Memories,* p. 44. The Sweet Medicine story is one of several oral traditions of the Cheyennes that tell how the chieftain system began among the tribe. A similar instruction was quoted by Dorsey in *The Cheyenne,* p. 14.

4. *Missouri Republican* (St. Louis), November 3, 1851.

5. George Armstrong Custer, *My Life on the Plains* (Norman: University of Oklahoma Press, 1962), pp. 362–63.

6. Edward W. Wynkoop's Unfinished Manuscript, Colorado Historical Society, pp. 27–28.

7. Garrard, *Wah-to-Yah,* pp. 48–49.

8. George E. Hyde, *Life of George Bent Written from His Letters,* ed. Savoie Lottinville (Norman: University of Oklahoma Press, 1967), p. 295.

9. *Report of the Commissioner of Indian Affairs, 1865,* p. 704.

10. Grinnell, *The Cheyenne Indians,* Vol. 1, pp. 336–37.

11. Wynkoop's Manuscript, p. 29.

12. Hyde, *Life of George Bent,* p. 323.

13. Henry M. Stanley, "A British Journalist Reports the Medicine Lodge Peace Councils of 1867," *Kansas Historical Quarterly,* Vol. 33, No. 3 (1967), p. 316.

14. *Missouri Republican* (Saint Louis), October 29, 1851.

15. Hyde, *Life of George Bent,* p. 324.

16. Stands In Timber and Liberty, *Cheyenne Memories,* p. 47.

17. Rodolphe Petter, *English-Cheyenne Dictionary* (Kettle Falls, Washington, 1915), pp. 230–31.

18. Custer, *My Life on the Plains,* p. 356.
19. Garrard, *Wah-to-Yah,* p. 51.

CHAPTER 2

1. A. P. Nasatir, *Before Lewis and Clark, Documents Illustrating the History of the Missouri, 1785–1804* (St. Louis: St. Louis Historical Documents Foundation, 1952), pp. 309–10.
2. Ibid., p. 296.
3. Elliott Coues, *History of the Expedition under the Command of Captains Lewis and Clark,* 4 vols. (New York: Francis P. Harper, 1893), Vol. 3, pp. 1181–91.
4. Charles Mackenzie, *The Missouri Indians, a Narrative of Four Trading Expeditions to the Missoui, 1804–1805–1806, for the North-West Company,* in Louis Francois Rodigue Mason, *Les Bourgeois de la Compagnie du Nord-Ouest* (Quebec: Impr. Generale A. Cote, 1889–90), pp. 376–80.
5. Alexander Henry and David Thompson, *New Light on the Early History of the Greater Northwest, the Manuscript Journals of Alexander Henry, Fur Trader for the Northwest Company, and of David Thompson, Official Geographer and Explorer of the Same Company, 1799–1814,* ed. Elliott Coues (New York: Francis P. Harper, 1897), pp. 377–78.
6. Henry's account of the ill-fated adoption ceremony mentions a "Chief of Wolves" but does not identify his tribe.
7. Henry and Thompson, *Journals,* pp. 383–84.
8. Edwin James, *An Account of an Expedition from Pittsburgh to the Rocky Mountains, 1819–1820,* ed. Reuben Gold Thwaites (Cleveland: Arthur H. Clark Co., 1905), pp. 198–201.
9. Ibid., pp. 208–209. Captain John R. Bell, *The Journal of Captain John R. Bell, Official Journalist for the Stephen H. Long Expedition to the Rocky Mountains, 1820,* Vol. 6 of *The Far West and the Rockies Historical Series, 1820–1875* ed. Harlin M. Fuller and LeRoy R. Hafen (Glendale: Arthur H. Clark Co., 1957), p. 192.
10. James, *Expedition,* p. 212.
11. The Treaty of 1825 gives his Sioux name of Sho-e-mow-e-to-chaw-ca-we-wah-ca-to-we. George Catlin indicated his name to be Nee-hee-o-ee-woo-tis, or Wolf on the Hill. *North American Indians,* 2 vols. (Edinburgh: Oliver and Boyd, 1926), Vol. 2 p. 2. George Bird Grinnell gave the Cheyenne name as Hoh-nih-ohka-i-yo-hos. *The Fighting Cheyennes* (Norman: University of Oklahoma Press, 1956), p. 221.
12. Russell Reid and Clell G. Cannon, eds., "Journal of the

Atkinson-O'Fallon Expedition," *North Dakota Historical Quarterly,* Vol. 4, No. 1 (1929), pp. 27–28.

13. Atkinson and O'Fallon's Report, November 7, 1825, in "Treaties with Several Tribes," *American State Papers,* Vol. 2, 19th Cong., 1st sess., No. 226 (1826), pp. 605–608.

14. *Daily National Intelligencer* (Washington, D.C.), November 4, 1825.

15. Catlin, *North American Indians,* Vol. 2, p. 2. Catlin also told of a Mandan chief's robe on which were depicted twelve battle scenes. The chief's verbal description of these battles, as translated to Catlin by James Kipp, included four in which the Mandan claimed to have killed Cheyennes. In one case, a Cheyenne chief sent word to the Mandan, Mah-to-toh-pa (Four Bears), that he wished to fight him. In an ensuing duel the Mandan killed the Cheyenne with a lance. In another fight Mah-to-toh-pa was badly wounded by bullets from the guns of twenty-five to thirty Cheyennes. A third scene depicted a Cheyenne chief dressed in war-eagle dress and carrying a beautiful shield ornamented with eagle quills. He was killed by the Mandan, along with the Cheyenne's wife who rushed out to help. Lastly, a duel was fought between Four Bears and a Cheyenne chief who challenged him. The duel was fought on horseback with guns at first, then with bows and arrows, and then, dismounted, the Mandan overcame the Cheyenne, killing him with his own knife and scalping him. Kipp, who had been among the Mandans for eight years as a trader, assured Catlin that these events had happened during his stay, thus between 1824 and 1832. Catlin, *North American Indians,* Vol. 1, pp. 166–73.

Another highly romanticized robe story with scant detail appeared in *Military and Naval Magazine of the United States.* This story tells of a Rocky Mountain Indian, possibly a Crow, whose girl friend was captured by a Cheyenne war party. The Indian hero of the tale followed the Cheyennes and rescued the girl, then returned with a large war party and killed all the Cheyennes but one, who was forced thereafter to live in disgrace. "A Tale of the Rocky Mountains," (September, 1835), pp. 32–39.

16. Kingsbury's account of the Dodge expedition states that the Cheyennes "had just killed their principal chief" and again specifies that "the Cheyennes having killed their principal chief, the High-Backed Wolf." Lieutenant G. P. Kingbury, "Report on the Expedition of Dragoons, Under Colonel Henry Dodge, to the Rocky Mountains in 1835," *American State Papers,* Military Affairs, Vol. 6, 24th Cong., 1st sess., No. 654, (1861), pp. 130–46. Ford's account states that "they had murdered their only Chief about one year ago." Louis Pelzer, "Captain Ford's Journal of an Expedition to the Rocky Mountains," *Mississippi Valley Historical Review,* Vol. 12, No. 4 (March, 1926), p. 567. This

would date his death as 1834. George Bent placed it at "about 1832." Hyde, *Life of George Bent,* p. 324. Grinnell stated that the daughters of High-Backed-Wolf said he died the year of star shower, which would be 1833 (the Leonid Shower of November 14), and that the Cheyennes said the stars fell from the sky because of the death of such an important man. Grinnell also cited White Bull as saying that High-Backed-Wolf, Limber Lance, and Bull Head visited Washington in 1832, the first Cheyenne delegation to do so, but so far no corroborating evidence has come to light. *The Cheyenne Indians,* Vol. 2, p. 30.

17. Hugh Evans, *Journal of Colonel Henry Dodge's Expedition to the Rocky Mountains in 1835,* ed. Fred S. Perrine, *Mississippi Valley Historical Review,* Vol. 14, No. 1 (June, 1927), p. 212.

18. Kingsbury, "Report on the Dodge Expedition," p. 140.

19. Ibid., pp. 140–41.

CHAPTER 3

1. Oh-kohm-kho-wais, Grinnell, *The Fighting Cheyennes,* p. 173; Okohm-e-ho-wist, Hyde, *Life of George Bent,* p. 294; O-cum-who-wurst, Garrard, *Wah-to-Yah,* p. 98, or O-cum-who-wust, p. 115. The correct translation of the name is really "Yellow Coyote."

2. George Bird Grinnell, "Bent's Old Fort and Its Builders," *Collections of the Kansas State Historical Society, 1919–22,* Vol. 15 (1922), p. 4.

3. Hyde, *Life of George Bent,* pp. 43–46.

4. William Clark To C. A. Harris, St. Louis, April 30, 1838, University of Oklahoma Division of Manuscripts, Berthrong Collection, Box 5, Folder 27.

5. Hyde, *Life of George Bent,* p. 72.

6. Grinnell, *The Fighting Cheyennes,* pp. 45–62.

7. Ibid., pp. 63–69. The death of the High-Backed Wolf in 1833 or 1834 places serious doubt on Grinnell's account of a High-Backed-Wolf being the leading chief in 1840, when the Cheyennes and Arapahoes made peace with the Kiowas and Comanches near Bent's Fort. There evidently was another High-Backed-Wolf later, a Northern Cheyenne who was killed at the Battle of the Platte Bridge in 1865. Hyde, *Life of George Bent,* p. 219.

8. Grinnell, *The Fighting Cheyennes,* pp. 75–77.

9. John Charles Frémont, *Report of the Exploring Expedition to the Rocky Mountains* (Ann Arbor: University Microfilms, 1966), p. 288. In August, 1860, a bloody battle between the Cheyennes and Delawares was fought on the Solomon River, one hundred miles above Fort Riley, with heavy Delaware losses reported. "Bypaths of Kansas History," *Kansas Historical Quarterly,* Vol. 7 (1938), p. 418.

10. LeRoy R. Hafen, ed., "The W. M. Boggs Manuscript About Bent's Fort, Kit Carson, the Far West and Life Among the Indians," *Colorado Magazine*, Vol. 7, No. 2 (1930), p. 53.

11. J. W. Abert, *Report of an Expedition Led by Lieut. Abert on the Upper Arkansas and Through the Country of the Comanche Indians, in the Fall of the Year 1845, Journal of Lieutenant J. W. Abert, from Bent's Fort to St. Louis in 1845, Senate Document No. 438*, 29th Cong., 1st sess. (1846), p. 5.

12. Ibid., p. 3.

13. J. W. Abert, *Report of Lieut. J. W. Abert of His Examination of New Mexico in the Years 1846–'47, Senate Executive Document No. 23*, 30th Cong., 1st sess. (1848), as found in W. H. Emory, *Notes of a Military Reconnaissance, from Fort Leavenworth, in Missouri, to San Diego, in California, House Executive Document No. 41*, 30th Cong., 1st sess. (1848), p. 422.

14. Fitzpatrick to Harvey, Bent's Fort, September 18, 1847, *Appendix to the Report of the Commissioner of Indian Affairs, 1847, Senate Executive Document No. 1*, 30th Cong., 1st sess., p. 242.

15. Garrard, *Wah-to-Yah*, pp. 98–99.

16. Ibid., p. 115.

17. George Frederick Ruxton, *Ruxton of the Rockies*, collected by Clyde and Mae Reed Porter (Norman: University of Oklahoma Press, 1950), p. 273.

18. Ibid., p. 180.

19. Garrard, *Wah-to-Yah*, p. 82.

20. Fitzpatrick, *Appendix to the Report*, p. 242.

21. Hafen, "The W. M. Boggs Manuscript," p. 52.

22. Slim Face's Indian name is given as "Vip-po-nah" by the Treaty of Medicine Lodge.

23. Rufus B. Sage, *Rocky Mountain Life or Startling Scenes and Perilous Adventures in the Far West* (Dayton: Edward Canby, 1859), p. 354.

24. Abert, *Examination of New Mexico*, pp. 423–24.

25. Garrard, *Wah-to-Yah*, p. 56.

26. Hyde, *Life of George Bent*, p. 326. This man has often been misidentified as Dull Knife. Quite likely George Bent was correct, however, for the oldest of the three in the photograph taken at Camp Supply could easily have been eighty. The fact that Vip-po-nah signed the Treaty of Medicine Lodge only a year and a half earlier gives support to Bent.

CHAPTER 4

1. Heskovizenako, or "Thorny Bear." Grinnell says that Porcupine Bear was shot in the thigh and lamed by a Shawnee during the 1844

fight with the Delawares and was thereafter known by some as "Lame Shawnee." *The Fighting Cheyennes,* p. 77.

2. James P. Beckwourth, *The Life and Adventures of James P. Beckwourth,* ed. T. D. Bonner (New York: Alfred A. Knopf, 1931), pp. 317–18.

3. Hyde, *Life of George Bent,* p. 338.

4. Grinnell, *The Fighting Cheyennes,* pp. 56–57.

5. Hyde, *Life of George Bent,* p. 338.

6. *Missouri Republican,* October 29, 1851.

7. The English names of the signers of the Treaty of Fort Laramie have never been identified by historians and writers. They were Wah-ha-nis-setta or Wah-a-nas-satta (He Who Walks With His Toes Turned Out), described as the "great medicine man of the tribe [who] has custody of the Medicine Arrows," *Missouri Republican,* November 3, 1851; Voist-ti-toe-vetz or Vois-ti-toe-vitz (White Cow); Nahk-ko-mein (Bear's Feather or Bark); and Koh-kah-y-wh-cum-est (probably White Crow, though possibly White Antelope). Documents Relating to Negotiations of Indian Treaties, 1801–69, Ratified Treaties.

Agent Thomas Twiss signed a treaty in 1859 with the Northern Cheyennes and listed both White Crow and White Cow as signers. *Proceedings of Council Held September 18, 1859, by Agent Thomas Twiss, Deer Creek, N.T., House Executive Document No. 61,* 36th Cong., 1st sess. (1860).

8. Nah-co-mense, Abert, *Examination of New Mexico,* p. 421.

9. Documents Relating to Negotiations of Indian Treaties, 1801–69, Ratified Treaties.

10. Beckwourth, *Life and Adventures,* pp. 296–97.

11. Abert, *Journal,* p. 4.

12. Ibid., p. 5.

13. Garrard, *Wah-to-Yah,* p. 86.

14. *Missouri Republican,* November 3, 1851.

15. Hyde, *Life of George Bent,* p. 48.

16. Henry C. Keeling, "My Experience with the Cheyenne Indians," *Chronicles of Oklahoma,* Vol. 3, No. 1 (1925), pp. 59–73.

17. Voi Vatosh, or He Who Moves on the Cloud, *Daily National Intelligencer,* January 7, 1851; Vaive-ah-toish, Rides on the Clouds, *New York Times,* October 30, 1851; Vaive atoish, Rides on the Clouds, Hiram Martin Chittenden and Alfred Talbot Richardson, *Life, Letters, and Travels of Father Pierre-Jean De Smet, S.J., 1801–1873,* 4 vols. (New York: Francis P. Harper, 1905), Vol. 2, p. 688. Other variations include Touches-the-Sky and Touching Cloud.

18. Grinnell, *The Fighting Cheyennes,* pp. 74, 78.

19. Ibid., pp. 74–75; Hyde, *Life of George Bent,* p. 91.

20. Grinnell, *The Fighting Cheyennes,* p. 80.

21. Chittenden and Richardson, *Life of De Smet,* p. 687.
22. *Missouri Republican,* October 30, 1851.
23. *Daily National Intelligencer,* November 19, December 1, 5, 12, 13, 1851; January 7, 8, 10, 1852.
24. Grinnell, *The Fighting Cheyennes,* p. 82.
25. He-vo-vi-tas-tami-utsts, or Moving Whirlwind, ibid., p. 104; Min-nin-ne-wah, C. J. Kappler, ed., *Indian Affairs: Laws and Treaties,* 4 vols. (1904, 1913, 1927), Vol. 2, p. 989.
26. Sage, *Rocky Mountain Life,* p. 334.
27. Hafen, "The W. M. Boggs Manuscript," p. 53.
28. Ibid., p. 55.
29. Grinnell, *The Fighting Cheyennes,* p. 102.
30. Ibid., pp. 19–20.
31. Ibid., pp. 103–104.
32. *Testimony Taken by a Select Committee of the Senate Concerning the Removal of the Northern Cheyenne Indians,* Senate Report No. 78, 46th Cong., 2d sess. (1880), p. 35.
33. Hyde, *Life of George Bent,* p. 357.
34. Berthrong, *The Southern Cheyennes,* p. 387.
35. Frederick Remington, "Artist Wanderings Among the Cheyennes," *Century Magazine* (May–October, 1889), p. 539.

CHAPTER 5

1. Vokivocum-mast, *New York Times,* October 30, 1851; Voki vokammast, Chittendon and Richardson, *Life of De Smet,* p. 688; Vo-ki-vokamast, Kappler, *Indian Affairs,* Vol. 2, p. 810; Wokai-hwo-ko-mas, Grinnell, *The Fighting Cheyennes,* p. 57.
2. Hyde, *Life of George Bent,* pp. 40–41.
3. Grinnell, *The Fighting Cheyennes,* pp. 64–65.
4. W. T. Hamilton, *My Sixty Years on the Plains, Trapping, Trading, and Indian Fighting,* ed. E. T. Sieber (Columbus: Long's College Book Co., 1951), p. 192.
5. Hafen, "The W. M. Boggs Manuscript," p. 50.
6. *New York Times,* October 30, 1851, citing *Missouri Republican.* It is possible that White Antelope may have been one of the four chiefs who signed the original treaty. "O-ko-ka" means "crow" in Cheyenne; "voki" means "antelope"; and "vo-cum-ni" means "white." One of the signatures on the treaty was Koh-kah-y-wh-cum-est. Probably this was White Crow.
7. Sumner to AAG, September 20, 1857, Records of the War Department, Office of the Adjutant General, Letters Received.
8. Grinnell, *The Fighting Cheyennes,* p. 155.

9. Colonel W. A. Phillips, "Kansas History," *Transactions of the Kansas State Historical Society, 1886–1888,* Vol. 4 (1890), pp. 352–53.
10. Kappler, *Indian Affairs,* Vol. 2, p. 810.
11. *The Daily Times* (Leavenworth), October 23, 1860.
12. Berthrong, *The Southern Cheyennes,* p. 155.
13. *Report of the Commissioner of Indian Affairs, 1863,* pp. 247–48.
14. "The Sand Creek Massacre," *Report of the Secretary of War, Senate Executive Document No. 26,* 39th Cong., 2d sess. (1867), pp. 213–17.
15. Hyde, *Life of George Bent,* p. 152. A soldier, Nathan Snyder, testified that he saw an American flag at the west end of the village. "Sand Creek Massacre," p. 77. John Smith, who was in the camp, also testified he saw Black Kettle raise the flag. Ibid., p. 128.
16. Ibid., p. 49.
17. Hyde, *Life of George Bent,* p. 219.
18. "Sand Creek Massacre," pp. 67, 73, 137–38.

CHAPTER 6

1. Avo-na-co, Kappler, *Indian Affairs,* Vol. 2, pp. 7, 810.
2. *Report of the Commissioner of Indian Affairs, 1851,* pp. 332–37.
3. Hyde, *Life of George Bent,* p. 98.
4. Bent's Fort, October 28, 1857, Records of the Office of Indian Affairs, Upper Arkansas Agency, Letters Received.
5. Kappler, *Indian Affairs,* Vol. 2, pp. 807–11.
6. *New York Tribune,* March 18, 1863, quoting *Leavenworth Times,* March 13, 1863.
7. March 27, 1863.
8. *Daily National Intelligencer,* March 28, 1863.
9. *Washington Evening Star,* March 27, 1863.
10. *Washington National Republican,* March 27, 1863.
11. Ibid.
12. *New York Tribune,* April 7, 1863.
13. *New York Times,* April 8, 1863.
14. Ibid.
15. Ibid., April 13, 1863.
16. Ibid., April 11, 1863.
17. Hyde, *Life of George Bent,* p. 132. Wynkoop stated in an affidavit: "Sergeant Fribbley was approached by Lean Bear, and accompanied by him into our column, leaving his warriors at some distance. A short time after Lean Bear reached our command he was killed, and fire opened upon his band." "The Chivington Massacre," *Report of the Joint Special Committee Appointed Under Resolution of March 3, 1865, Senate Report No. 156,* 39th Cong., 2d sess. (1867), p. 75.

CHAPTER 7

1. Hyde, *Life of George Bent,* p. 338.
2. "Sand Creek Massacre," p. 103.
3. O-to-ah-nac-co, Kappler, *Indian Affairs,* Vol. 2, p. 989.
4. "Sand Creek Massacre," pp. 216–17.
5. Ibid., p. 217.
6. Tall Bull probably signed the amended treaty at Fort Zarah, Kansas, November 20, 1866.
7. Berthrong, *The Southern Cheyennes,* p. 264.
8. Henry M. Stanley, *My Early Travels and Adventures in America and Asia,* 2 vols. (New York: Charles Scribner's Sons, 1905), Vol. 1, p. 29.
9. *New York Tribune,* October 23, 1867.
10. *Cincinnati Gazette,* October 21, 1867.
11. *Chicago Tribune,* October 24, 1867; *Missouri Republican,* October 22, 1867.
12. *Cincinnati Commercial,* October 24, 1867.
13. Ibid., November 4, 1867.
14. *New York Tribune,* November 8, 1867.
15. *Chicago Tribune,* November 4, 1867.
16. O-to-ah-has-tis, Kappler, *Indian Affairs,* Vol. 2, p. 989; Hotu-a-e-kha-ash-tait, Grinnell, *The Fighting Cheyennes,* p. 86.
17. *Cincinnati Commercial,* October 24, 1867.
18. Ibid., November 4, 1867.
19. Douglas C. Jones, *The Treaty of Medicine Lodge* (Norman: University of Oklahoma Press, 1966), pp. 84–85.
20. *Kansas Weekly Tribune,* (Lawrence), October 24, 1867.
21. *Missouri Republican,* October 24, 1867.
22. *Chicago Tribune,* November 4, 1867.
23. *Report of the Commissioner of Indian Affairs, 1868,* pp. 64–66.
24. Berthrong, *The Southern Cheyennes,* p. 309.
25. Ibid., p. 324.
26. Ibid., p. 340.
27. Ibid., pp. 340–44.
28. Ibid., p. 351.
29. John H. Seger, *Early Days Among the Cheyenne and Arapahoe Indians* (Norman: University of Oklahoma Press, 1956), p. 34. Bull Bear's son attended Carlisle school in Pennsylvania, taking a five-year course in printing which he chose as his profession. He also adopted the white man's name "Richard Davis." *Cheyenne Transporter* (Darlington Agency, I.T.), June 26, 1886.
30. *Kansas Daily Tribune* (Lawrence), October 12, 1872.
31. Robert Hamilton, "Early Days in Kingfisher County," *The Chronicles of Oklahoma,* Vol. 18, No. 2 (1940), pp. 185–89.

32. Remington, "Artist Wanderings," p. 539.

33. Voh-kin-ne, "Report of a Council held at Fort Zarah, Kansas, November 10th, 1866, with the Cheyenne and Arapaho Indians of the Upper Arkansas Agency," Records of the Bureau of Indian Affairs.

34. Indian Agent Simeon Whiteley testified in 1865 that he had received word from the Northern Arapahoes that this Roman Nose was dead. "Sand Creek Massacre," p. 218.

35. Wynkoop to Cooley, August 14, 1866, Records of the Bureau of Indian Affairs Upper Arkansas Agency, Letters Received.

36. George A. Forsyth, *Thrilling Days in Army Life* (New York: Harper & Brothers, 1901), p. 56, citing *Army Sacrifices*, by General Fry.

37. Theodore Davis, "A Summer on the Plains," *Harper's New Monthly Magazine*, Vol. 36, No. 18 (1868), p. 295.

38. Hyde, *Life of George Bent*, p. 306.

39. Ibid., pp. 219–21; Berthrong, *The Southern Cheyennes*, pp. 248–49.

40. Berthrong, *The Southern Cheyennes*, pp. 254–55; Hyde, *Life of George Bent*, pp. 239–40.

41. Hyde, *Life of George Bent*, p. 243.

42. "Report of Council at Fort Zarah," Records of the Bureau of Indian Affairs.

43. Hyde, *Life of George Bent*, p. 259.

44. Ibid.

45. Ibid., p. 260.

46. *The Chicago Times*, October 22, 1867.

47. Hyde, *Life of George Bent*, p. 303.

48. *New York Herald*, October 12, 1868.

49. Hyde, *Life of George Bent*, p. 303.

50. Sigmund Schlesinger, "The Beecher Island Fight," *Collections of the Kansas State Historical Society, 1919–1922* Vol. XV (1923), p. 546.

51. Hyde, *Life of George Bent*, p. 306.

CHAPTER 8

1. Mo-ta-vato, Kappler, *Indian Affairs,* Vol. 2, p. 810; Moke-ta-ve-to, ibid., p. 891; Moke-tav-a-to, ibid., p. 989; Moke-to-ve-to, "Report of Council at Fort Zarah," Records of the Bureau of Indian Affairs; Moka-ta-va-tah, Wynkoop's Manuscript, p. 31. J. R. Mead, an early trader at the site of Wichita, Kansas, met Black Kettle at the mouth of the Little Arkansas River in 1866. Mead described the Cheyenne head chief as a "mild, peaceable, pleasant, good man, past middle life." Black Kettle claimed that his hand had never been raised against a white man, woman, or child. *Wichita Eagle,* March 3, 1893.

2. *Missouri Republican,* October 22, 1867.

3. *New York Times,* December 24, 1868.

4. George Bent to Colonel Tappan, March 16, 1889, three unpublished letters, Colorado Historical Society. In Hyde, *Life of George Bent,* p. 322, Black Kettle's age at death is given as sixty-seven.

5. Hyde, *Life of George Bent,* p. 322.

6. Grinnell, *The Cheyenne Indians,* Vol. 1, p. 91.

7. Hyde, *Life of George Bent,* p. 323.

8. Grinnell, *The Fighting Cheyennes,* p. 92.

9. Hyde, *Life of George Bent,* p. 102.

10. Ibid., p. 323.

11. The Cheyenne spelling of Black Kettle's name on the first version of the treaty was Me-tu-ra-to.

12. "Sand Creek Massacre," p. 103.

13. Boone to Dole, January 18, 1862, Records of the Bureau of Indian Affairs, Upper Arkansas Agency, Letters Received.

14. *Report of the Commissioner of Indian Affairs, 1863,* pp. 247–48.

15. Hyde, *Life of George Bent,* p. 132.

16. "Sand Creek Massacre," p. 169.

17. Ibid., p. 31.

18. Ibid., pp. 30–31.

19. Wynkoop's Manuscript, pp. 30–31.

20. Ibid., p. 29.

21. "Sand Creek Massacre," p. 33.

22. Ibid., p. 44.

23. Ibid., p. 213.

24. Though he did visit Denver, it is not true, as stated by George Bent (Hyde, *Life of George Bent,* p. 131) and many other historians, that Black Kettle ever visited Washington, D.C.

25. "Sand Creek Massacre," p. 103.

26. Hyde, *Life of George Bent,* p. 155.

27. *Report of the Commissioner of Indian Affairs, 1865,* pp. 704–705.

28. Hyde, *Life of George Bent,* p. 248.

29. Kappler, *Indian Affairs,* Vol. 2, p. 891.

30. Hyde, *Life of George Bent,* p. 251; Wynkoop to Pope, March 12, 1866, Records of the Bureau of Indian Affairs Upper Arkansas Agency, Letters Received.

31. Wynkoop to Cooley, Fort Ellsworth, August 14, 1866, Records of the Office of Indian Affairs, Upper Arkansas Agency, Letters Received.

32. "Report of Council at Fort Zarah," Records of the Bureau of Indian Affairs.

33. Hyde, *Life of George Bent,* p. 278.

34. Ibid., pp. 278–81.

35. *Chicago Tribune,* September 30, 1867.
36. *New York Tribune,* October 23, 1867.
37. Jones, *Treaty of Medicine Lodge,* p. 73.
38. Stanley, "Medicine Lodge Peace Councils," p. 268.
39. Ibid., p. 291.
40. Jones, *Treaty of Medicine Lodge,* pp. 137–41.
41. Ibid., p. 206.
42. *New York Tribune,* November 8, 1867.
43. Stanley, "Medicine Lodge Peace Councils," p. 315.
44. Fort Hays, Letters Sent, August 6, 1868.
45. *Kansas Daily Tribune,* August 14, 1868.
46. "Report of an Interview between Colonel E. W. Wynkoop, United States Indian Agent, and Little Rock, a Cheyenne Chief, held at Fort Larned, Kansas, August 19, 1868," *Report of the Commissioner of Indian Affairs, 1868,* p. 72.
47. Alvord to Roy, Old Fort Cobb, October 30, 1868, Records of the War Department, Office of the Adjutant General, Letters Received.
48. "Report of a Conversation held between Colonel and Bvt. Major General W. B. Hazen, U.S.A., on special service, and Chiefs of the Cheyenne and Arapahoe Tribes of Indians at Fort Cobb, Indian Territory, November 20, 1868," Records of the War Department Office of the Adjutant General, Letters Received.
49. Moving Behind, a Cheyenne woman, later stated: "There was a sharp curve in the river where an old road-crossing used to be. Indian men used to go there to water their ponies. Here we saw the bodies of Black Kettle and his wife, lying under the water. The horse they had ridden lay dead beside them. We observed that they had tried to escape across the river when they were shot." Theodore A. Ediger and Vinnie Hoffman, "Some Reminiscences of the Battle of the Washita," *The Chronicles of Oklahoma,* Vol. 33, No. 2 (1955), p. 140.
50. Sheridan to Sherman, Chicago, November 1, 1869, *Annual Report of the Secretary of War, 1869–70,* p. 47.
51. *New York Times,* December 22, 1868.
52. E. Adamson Hoebel, *The Cheyennes, Indians of the Great Plains* (New York: Henry Holt and Co., 1960), pp. 47, 70.

CHAPTER 9

1. Grinnell, *The Cheyenne Indians,* Vol. 2, p. 51.
2. Tah-me-la-pach-me (Arapaho name), Kappler, *Indian Affairs,* Vol. 2. p. 1015; Wo-he-hiv, Grinnell, *The Fighting Cheyennes,* p. 46.
3. Oh-cum-ga-che (Arapaho name), Kappler, *Indian Affairs,* Vol. 2, p. 1015; Okohm-ha-ka, Hyde, *Life of George Bent,* p. 250; Okohm-ha-

ket ibid., p. 294. There was also a Southern Cheyenne Chief Little Wolf, who signed the Treaty of Fort Wise in 1861 as O-ne-a-ha-ket, Kappler, *Indian Affairs,* Vol. 2, p. 810. George Bent spent some time with the band of this chief and gave his name as Honi-a-ha-ka, Hyde, *Life of George Bent,* p. 250.

4. *Report of the Commissioner of Indian Affairs, 1856,* pp. 638–54.

5. Alban W. Hoopes, "Thomas S. Twiss, Indian Agent on the Upper Platte, 1855–61," *Mississippi Valley Historical Review,* Vol. 20 (1933–34), pp. 353–64.

6. George E. Hyde, *Red Cloud's Folk* (Norman: University of Oklahoma Press, 1937), pp. 138–39.

7. Hyde, *Life of George Bent,* pp. 342–43.

8. Other chiefs present were Pretty Bear, Little Moon, Man-That-Stands-on-the-Ground, Rabbit-That-Jumps, Bob Tail, Dead White Leg, and the Brave Soldier. Charles Edmund DeLand, "The Sioux Wars," *South Dakota Historical Collections,* Vol. 15 (1930), p. 67.

9. Hyde, *Red Cloud's Folk,* pp. 142–43.

10. Grinnell, *The Fighting Cheyennes,* p. 234.

11. Ibid., p. 238.

12. Hyde, *Life of George Bent,* p. 346. Some writers give Little Wolf credit for the burning of Fort Fetterman.

13. *United States Statutes at Large,* Vol. 15, p. 655.

14. *The Evening Star* (Washington, D.C.), November 3, 1873.

15. The other chiefs were Strong Wolf, Black Hawk, Spotted Wolf, Lame White Man, Wolf-Who-Has-Lain-Down, and White Powder. Ibid., November 8, 1873.

16. *New York Times,* November 14, 1873.

17. *The Evening Star,* November 14, 1873.

18. Grinnell, *The Fighting Cheyennes,* pp. 359–82.

19. *New York Times,* April 22, 1877.

20. *Testimony Concerning Removal,* p. 58; Grinnell, *The Fighting Cheyennes,* p. 400.

21. Grinnell, *The Fighting Cheyennes,* p. 401.

22. *Testimony Concerning Removal,* pp. 4–5, 25, 47.

23. John Miles to John Mizner, September 20, 1878, University of Oklahoma Division of Manuscripts, Walter S. Campbell Collection.

24. *Report of the Secretary of War, 1878,* p. 46.

25. Peter M. Wright, "The Pursuit of Dull Knife from Fort Reno in 1878–79," *The Chronicles of Oklahoma,* Vol. 46, No. 2 (1968), p. 147.

26. Grinnell, *The Fighting Cheyennes,* pp. 407–408.

27. *New York Times,* October 5, 1878.

28. Ibid., October 15, 1878.

29. Ibid., October 26, 27, 1878.

30. Grinnell, *The Fighting Cheyennes,* pp. 411–13.

31. Stands In Timber and Liberty, *Cheyenne Memories,* p. 235.
32. *Testimony Concerning Removal,* p. 12.
33. *New York Times,* September 28, 1879.
34. Grinnell, *The Fighting Cheyennes,* p. 427.
35. Kuc-kun-ni-wi, Bureau of American Ethnology Catalogue Card. There was another chief named Little Chief who was prominent among the Southern Cheyennes at this same time.
36. Peter J. Powell, *Sweet Medicine,* 2 vols. (Norman: University of Oklahoma Press, 1969), p. 278.
37. *Testimony Concerning Removal,* pp. VI–XI.
38. Ibid.
39. Ibid., Little Chief and Ben Clark passed through Caldwell on their return from Washington. The Caldwell (Kansas) *Commercial* commented: "Little Chief is a man of about 50 years of age, tall, and of commanding appearance, and Indian though he be has more brain power than some of the white milksops the newspapers advertise as great statesmen. If we could only place a few Little Chiefs into Congress, it is possible the Indian question would be solved." September 1, 1881.
40. Ibid.
41. Ibid.
42. *Report of the Commissioner of Indian Affairs, 1881,* 1–1ii.
43. Powell, *Sweet Medicine,* pp. 283–84.
44. *Report of the Commissioner of Indian Affairs, 1882,* p. 35.
45. Powell, *Sweet Medicine,* pp. 413–14.

CHAPTER 10

1. Hark-kah-o-me, Treaty of Little Arkansas, Kappler, *Indian Affairs,* p. 892; Hah-ket-home-mah, Treaty of Medicine Lodge, Ibid., p. 989; Tah-ke-ome, 1873 Agreement, *House Executive Document No. 12,* 43d Cong., 1st sess., pp. 2–3.
2. Hubert E. Collins, *Warpath and Cattle Trail,* (New York: William Morrow & Co., 1928), p. 225.
3. Grinnell, *The Fighting Cheyennes,* p. 84.
4. *Report of the Commissioner of Indian Affairs, 1863,* pp. 128–30.
5. *Kansas Daily Tribune,* October 5, 1867.
6. Hyde, *Life of George Bent,* p. 244.
7. Ibid., p. 252; Berthrong, *The Southern Cheyennes,* pp. 258–59.
8. *Missouri Republican,* November 2, 1867; Kappler, *Indian Affairs,* p. 989.
9. Sheridan to Nichols, January 1, 1869, University of Oklahoma Division of Manuscripts, Sheridan Papers.

10. Ibid.

11. *New York Times,* May 24, 25, 26, June 1, 1871; Berthrong, *The Southern Cheyennes,* p. 362.

12. Hyde, *Life of George Bent,* p. 255.

13. Berthrong, *The Southern Cheyennes,* pp. 375–78, 384.

14. *House Executive Document No. 12,* pp. 2–3.

15. *Washington Evening Star,* November 14, 1873.

16. *Wichita Eagle,* July 9, 1874; *Kansas Daily Tribune,* October 28, 1874; Berthrong, *The Southern Cheyennes,* p. 392.

17. Berthrong, *The Southern Cheyennes,* pp. 389–90.

18. *Wichita Eagle,* August 2, 1877.

19. Ho-ho-man-muck-si, 1873 Agreement, *House Executive Document No. 12,* p. 3.

20. Hyde, *Life of George Bent,* p. 290–94.

21. *Kansas Daily Tribune,* April 12, 1870.

22. Ibid., April 13, 1870.

23. William Nicholson, "A Tour of Indian Agencies in Kansas and the Indian Territory," *Kansas Historical Quarterly,* Vol. 3, No. 4 (November, 1934), p. 348.

24. Berthrong, *The Southern Cheyennes,* pp. 392–63.

25. Ibid., p. 373.

26. *Winfield Courier,* April 10, 1873.

27. Berthrong, *The Southern Cheyennes,* p. 385.

28. Hyde, *Life of George Bent,* p. 360.

29. Berthrong, *The Southern Cheyennes,* pp. 396–400.

30. Donald J. Berthrong, *The Cheyenne and Arapaho Ordeal* (Norman: University of Oklahoma Press, 1976), p. 18.

31. Ibid., pp. 97–101.

32. Ibid., p. 109.

33. Ibid., pp. 113–15, 127.

34. November 2, 1885.

35. Ma-nim-ic, Wynkoop manuscript; Mun-a-men-ek, Report of Council Held at Fort Zarah, November 10, 1866 (Berthrong Collection); Menimick, Account of Meeting Between Quakers and Indians at Camp Supply, April 22, 1870, Records of the Office of Indian Affairs, Central Superintendency, 1868–70, Letters Received; Minnimic, *Wichita Eagle,* April 25, 1878; Mun-a-men-ek, Treaty of Little Arkansas.

36. Wynkoop's Manuscript.

37. Stan Hoig, *The Sand Creek Massacre,* (Norman: University of Oklahoma Press, 1961), pp. 99–104.

38. Kappler, *Indian Affairs,* pp. 887–89.

39. *Kansas Weekly Tribune,* October 31, 1867.

40. Berthrong, *The Southern Cheyennes,* p. 339.

41. Account of Meeting Between Quakers and Indians at Camp Supply, April 22, 1870, Records of the Office of Indian Affairs, Central Superintendency, 1868–70, Letters Received.

42. Ibid.

43. Hyde, *Life of George Bent,* p. 359.

44. Ibid., pp. 365–66; *Wichita Eagle,* April 15, 1875; *Report of the Commissioner of Indian Affairs, 1875,* pp. 49, 269.

45. *Wichita Eagle,* May 6, 13, 20, 1875.

46. Ibid., May 22, 1875.

47. Ibid., April 25, 1878.

48. Ibid.

49. Ibid., January 20, 1879.

Bibliography

ARCHIVAL MATERIALS

Colorado State Historical Society. Edward W. Wynkoop's Unfinished Manuscript.
Colorado State Historical Society. Three letters from George Bent to Colonel Samuel Tappan.
Oklahoma State Historical Society. Cheyenne and Arapaho Agency Files.
University of Oklahoma Division of Manuscripts. Berthrong Collection.
———. Walter S. Campbell Collection.
———. The Duke Collection, American Indian Oral History, American Indian Institute.
———. Sheridan Papers.

ARTICLES

"Bypaths of Kansas History." *Kansas Historical Quarterly,* Vol. 7 (1938).
"Bypaths of Kansas History." *Kansas Historical Quarterly,* Vol. 10 (1941).
Collings, Ellsworth. "Roman Nose: Chief of the Cheyenne." *The Chronicles of Oklahoma,* Vol. 42, No. 4 (1964–65).
Covington, James Warren. "Causes of the Dull Knife Raid." *The Chronicles of Oklahoma,* Vol. 26, No. 1 (1948).
Davis, Theodore. "A Summer on the Plains." *Harper's New Monthly Magazine,* Vol. 36, No. 18 (1868).
DeLand, Charles Edmund. "The Sioux Wars." *South Dakota Historical Collections,* Vol. 15 (1930).
Ediger, Theodore A. and Hoffman, Vinnie. "Some Reminiscences of The Battle of the Washita." *The Chronicles of Oklahoma,* Vol. 33, No. 22 (1955).
Gage, Duane. "Black Kettle: A Noble Savage?" *The Chronicles of Oklahoma,* Vol. 45, No. 3 (1967).
Grinnell, George Bird. "Bent's Old Fort and Its Builders." *Collections of the Kansas State Historical Society, 1919–22,* Vol. 15 (1922).
Hafen, LeRoy R., ed. "The W. M. Boggs Manuscript About Bent's Fort,

Kit Carson, the Far West and Life Among the Indians." *Colorado Magazine,* Vol. 7, No. 2 (1930).

Hamilton, Robert. "Early Days in Kingfisher County." *The Chronicles of Oklahoma,* Vol. 18, No. 2 (1940).

Hill, Burton S. "The Great Indian Treaty Council of 1851." *Nebraska History,* Vol. 47, No. 1 (1966).

Hoopes, Alban W. "Thomas S. Twiss, Indian Agent on the Upper Platte, 1855–1861." *Mississippi Valley Historical Review,* Vol. 20 (1933–34).

Keeling, Henry C. "My Experiences with the Cheyenne Indians." *Chronicles of Oklahoma,* Vol. 3, No. 1 (April, 1925).

"Letter from J. W. McNeal, Guthrie, January 4, 1906, concerning the Dull Knife–Little Wolf Outbreak." *Transactions of the Kansas State Historical Society, 1905–1906,* Vol. 9 (1906).

"Letters Concerning the Presbyterian Mission in the Pawnee Country, near Bellvue, Neb., 1831–1849. Letters from Rev. John Dunbar, September 6, 1831, to May, 1849." *Collections of the Kansas State Historical Society, 1915–18,* Vol. 14 (1918).

"Military Operation, Cheyenne Expedition—Three Letters from Col. E. V. Sumner regarding his Expedition against the Cheyennes in August, 1857." *Transactions of the Kansas State Historical Society, 1889–1896,* Vol. 5 (1896).

Montgomery, Mrs. Frank C. "Fort Wallace and Its Relation to the Frontier." *Collections of the Kansas State Historical Society, 1926–28,* Vol. 17 (1928).

————. "Jacques D'Église on the Upper Missouri, 1791–1795." *Mississippi Valley Historical Review,* Vol. 14, No. 1 (1927).

Nasatir, Abraham P. "Anglo-Spanish Rivalry on the Upper Missoui." *Mississippi Valley Historical Review,* Vol. 16, No. 3 (1929).

Nicholson, William. "A Tour of Indian Agencies in Kansas and the Indian Territory." *Kansas Historical Quarterly,* Vol. 13, No. 4 (November, 1934).

Parker, Donald D. "Early Explorations and Fur Trading in South Dakota." *South Dakota Historical Collections and Report,* Vol. 25, (1950).

Peck, Robert Morris. "Recollections of Early Times in Kansas Territory." *Transactions of the Kansas State Historical Society, 1903–1904,* Vol. 8 (1904).

Peery, Dan W. "The Indians' Friend, John H. Seger." *The Chronicles of Oklahoma,* Vol. 10, No. 3 (1932).

Pelzer, Louis. "Captain Ford's Journal of an Expedition to the Rocky Mountains." *Mississippi Valley Historical Review,* Vol. 12, No. 4 (March, 1926).

Phillips, Colonel W. A. "Kansas History." *Transactions of the Kansas State Historical Society, 1886–1888,* Vol. 4 (1890).

Bibliography

Rees, D. S. "An Indian Fight on the Solomon." *Transactions of the Kansas State Historical Society, 1901–1902,* Vol. 7 (1902).

Reid, Russel, and Gannon, Clell G., eds. "Journal of the Atkinson-O'Fallon Expedition." *North Dakota Historical Quarterly,* Vol. 4, No. 1 (1929).

Remington, Frederick. "Artist Wanderings Among the Cheyennes." *Century Magazine,* May–October, 1889.

Schlesinger, Sigmund. "The Beecher Island Fight." *Collections of the Kansas State Historical Society, 1919–1922,* Vol XV (1923).

Stanley, Henry M. "A British Journalist Reports the Medicine Lodge Peace Councils of 1867." *Kansas Historical Quarterly,* Vol. 33, No. 3 (1967).

"A Tale of the Rocky Mountains." *Military and Naval Magazine of the United States,* September, 1835.

Will George F. "The Cheyenne Indians in North Dakota." *Proceedings of the Mississippi Valley Historical Association for the Year 1913–14,* Vol. 7 (1914).

Wilson, Hill P. "Black Kettle's Last Raid." *Collections of the Kansas State Historical Society, 1903–1904,* Vol. 8 (1904).

Woodward, George A. "Experiences with the Cheyenne Indians." *A Monthly Review of Military and Naval Affairs,* Vol. 1, No. 2 (April, 1879).

Wright, Peter M. "The Pursuit of Dull Knife from Fort Reno in 1878–1879." *The Chronicles of Oklahoma,* Vol. 46, No. 2 (1968).

Wynkoop, Edward E. "Edward Wanshear Wynkoop." *Collections of the Kansas State Historical Society, 1913–14,* Vol. 13 (1915).

BOOKS

Abel, Annie Heloise. *Tabeau's Narrative of Loisel's Expedition to the Upper Missouri.* Translated by Rose Abel Wright. Norman: University of Oklahoma Press, 1939.

Beckwourth, James P. *The Life and Adventures of James P. Beckwourth.* Edited by T. D. Bonner. New York: Alfred A. Knopf, 1931.

Bell, Captain John R. *The Journal of Captain John R. Bell, Official Journalist for the Stephen H. Long Expedition to the Rocky Mountains, 1820.* The Far West and the Rockies Historical Series, 1820–1875, edited and with introductions by Harlin M. Fuller and LeRoy R. Hafen, Vol. 6. Glendale: Arthur H. Clark Co., 1957.

Berthrong, Donald J. *The Cheyenne and Arapaho Ordeal.* Norman: University of Oklahoma Press, 1976.

———. *The Southern Cheyennes.* Norman: University of Oklahoma Press, 1963.

181

Bushnell, David I., Jr. *Villages of the Algonquian, Siouan, and Caddoan Tribes West of the Mississippi,* Bureau of Ethnology Bulletin No. 77. Washington: Government Printing Office, 1922.

Carter, Clarence Edwin, comp. and ed. *The Territorial Papers of the United States.* Washington: Government Printing Office, 1934-48.

Carvalho, S. N. *Incidents of Travel and Adventure in the Far West with Colonel Frémont's Last Expedition Across the Rocky Mountains.* New York: Derby & Jackson, 1857.

Catlin, George. *North American Indians.* 2 vols. Edinburgh: Oliver and Boyd, 1926.

Chittenden, Hiram Martin and Richardson, Alfred Talbot. *Life, Letters, and Travels of Father Pierre-Jean De Smet, S. J., 1801-1873.* 4 vols. New York: Francis P. Harper, 1905.

Collins, Dennis. *The Indians' Last Fight, or The Dull Knife Raid.* Girard, Kans.: Press of the Appeal to Reason, 1915.

Collins, Hubert E. *Warpath and Cattle Trail.* Foreword by Hamlin Garland. New York: William Morrow & Co., 1928.

Coues, Elliott. *History of the Expedition under the Command of Captains Lewis and Clark.* 4 vols. New York: Francis P. Harper, 1893.

Custer, George Armstrong. *My Life on the Plains.* Norman: University of Oklahoma Press, 1962.

Donaldson, Thomas. *The George Catlin Indian Gallery in the U.S. National Museum,* from the *Smithsonian Report of 1885.* Washington: Government Printing Office, 1887.

Dorsey, George A. *The Cheyenne.* Field Columbia Museum Publication 99, Anthology Series, Vol. 9, No. 1. Chicago, March, 1905.

Evans, Hugh. *Journal of Colonel Henry Dodge's Expedition to the Rocky Mountains in 1835.* Edited by Fred S. Perrine. *Mississippi Valley Historical Review,* Vol. 14, No. 1 (June, 1927).

Forsyth, George A. *Thrilling Days in Army Life.* New York: Harper & Brothers, 1901.

Fowler, Jacob. *The Journal of Jacob Fowler.* Edited by Elliott Coues. New York: Francis P. Harper, 1898.

Frémont, John Charles. *Narrative of Exploration and Adventure.* Edited by Allan Nevins. New York: Longmans, Green & Co., 1956.

———. *Report of the Exploring Expedition to the Rocky Mountains.* Ann Arbor: University Microfilms, 1966.

Garrard, Lewis H. *Wah-to-Yah and the Taos Trail.* Norman: University of Oklahoma Press, 1955.

Grinnell, George Bird. *By Cheyenne Campfires.* New Haven: Yale University Press, 1926.

———. *The Cheyenne Indians: Their History and Ways of Life.* 2 vols. New Haven: Yale University Press, 1923.

———. *The Fighting Cheyennes.* Norman: University of Oklahoma Press, 1956.

Hafen, LeRoy R. and Young, Francis Marion. *Fort Laramie and the Pageant of the West.* Glendale: Arthur H. Clark Co., 1938.

Hamilton, W. T. "Bill." *My Sixty Years on the Plains, Trapping, Trading, and Indian Fighting.* Edited by E. T. Sieber. Columbus: Long's College Book Co., 1951.

Henry, Alexander and Thompson, David. *New Light on the Early History of the Greater Northwest, the Manuscript Journals of Alexander Henry, Fur Trader for the Northwest Company, and of David Thompson, Official Geographer and Explorer of the Same Company, 1799–1814.* Edited by Elliott Coues. New York: Francis P. Harper, 1897.

Hodge, Frederick W. *Handbook of American Indians North of Mexico,* Bureau of American Ethnology Bulletin No. 30. Washington: Government Printing Office, 1910.

Hoebel, E. Adamson. *The Cheyennes: Indians of the Great Plains.* New York: Henry Holt & Co., 1960.

Hoig, Stan. *The Sand Creek Massacre.* Norman: University of Oklahoma Press, 1961.

Hyde, George E. *Life of George Bent Written from His Letters.* Edited by Savoie Lottinville. Norman: University of Oklahoma Press, 1967.

———.*Red Cloud's Folk.* Norman: University of Oklahoma Press, 1937.

Jablow, Joseph. *The Cheyenne in Plains Indian Trade Relations, 1795–1840.* New York: J. J. Augstin, 1951.

James, Edwin. *An Account of an Expedition, from Pittsburg to the Rocky Mountains 1819–1820.* Edited by Reuben Gold Thwaites. Cleveland: Arthur H. Clark Co., 1905.

Jones, Douglas C. *The Treaty of Medicine Lodge.* Norman: University of Oklahoma Press, 1966.

Llewellyn, K. N. and Hoebel, E. Adamson. *The Cheyenne Way: Conflict and Case Law in Primitive Jurisprudence.* Norman: University of Oklahoma Press, 1941.

Mackenzie, Charles. *The Missouri Indians, A Narrative of Four Trading Expeditions to the Missouri, 1804–1805–1806, for the North-West Company,* Louis François Rodique Masson, *Les Bourgeois de la Compagnie du Nord-Ouest.* Quebec: Impr. Generale A. Cote, 1889–1890.

Nasatir, A. P. *Before Lewis and Clark: Documents Illustrating the History of the Missouri, 1785–1804.* Saint Louis: Saint Louis Historical Documents Foundation, 1952.

Petter, Rodolphe. *English-Cheyenne Dictionary.* Kettle Falls, Washington, 1915.

Powell, Peter J. *Sweet Medicine.* 2 vols. Norman: University of Oklahoma Press, 1969.

Ruxton, George Frederick. *Life in the Far West.* Edited by LeRoy R. Hafen. Norman: University of Oklahoma Press, 1951.

————. *Ruxton of the Rockies*. Collected by Clyde Porter and Mae Reed Porter. Norman: University of Oklahoma Press, 1950.

Sage, Rufus, B. *Rocky Mountain Life, or Startling Scenes and Perilous Adventures in the Far West*. Dayton: Edward Canby, 1859.

————.*Rufus B. Sage, His Letters and Papers, 1836–1847*. Vol. 5 of *The Far West and the Rockies Historical Series*. Notes by LeRoy R. Hafen and Ann W. Hafen. Glendale: Arthur H. Clark Co., 1956.

Seger, John H. *Early Days Among the Cheyenne and Arapahoe Indians*. Norman: University of Oklahoma Press, 1956.

Stands In Timber, John, and Liberty, Margot, with the assistance of Robert M. Utley. *Cheyenne Memories*. New Haven: Yale University Press, 1967.

Stanley, Henry M. *My Early Travels and Adventures in America and Asia*. 2 vols. New York: Charles Scribner's Sons, 1905.

Thwaites, Reuben Gold, ed. *Bradbury's Travels in the Interior of America, 1809–1811*. Vol. 5 of *Early Western Travels 1748–1846*. Cleveland: Arthur H. Clark Co., 1904.

————. *Original Journals of the Lewis and Clark Expedition, 1804–1806, Printed from the Original Manuscripts ... and the Journals of Charles Floyd and Joseph Whitehouse*. 7 vols. New York: Dodd, Mead & Co., 1904.

GOVERNMENT DOCUMENTS

PUBLISHED

Abert, J. W. *Report of an Expedition Led by Lieut. Abert on the Upper Arkansas and Through the Country of the Comanche Indians, in the Fall of the Year 1845, Journal of Lieutenant J. W. Abert, from Bent's Fort to St. Louis in 1845*. Senate Document No. 438. 29th Cong., 1st sess. (1846).

————. *Report of Lieut. J. W. Abert of His Examination of New Mexico in the Years 1846–'47*. Senate Executive Document No. 23, 30th Cong., 1st sess. (1848), as found in W. H. Emory, *Notes of a Military Reconnaissance, from Fort Leavenworth, in Missouri, to San Diego, in California*. House Executive Document No. 41, 30th Cong., 1st sess (1848).

Annual Report of the Secretary of War, 1869–70.

Appendix to the Report of the Commissioner of Indian Affairs, 1847. Senate Executive Document No. 1, 30th Cong., 1st sess.

"The Chivington Massacre." *Report of the Joint Special Committee Appointed Under Resolution of March 3, 1865*. Senate Report No. 156, 39th Cong., 2d sess. (1867). "Articles of agreement with Cheyennes," House Executive Document No. 12, 43d Cong., 1st sess. (1873).

Kappler, C. J., comp. and ed. *Indian Affairs: Laws and Treaties.* 4 vols., 1904, 1913, 1927.

Kingsbury, Lieutenant G. P. "Report on the Expedition of Dragoons, Under Colonel Henry Dodge, to the Rocky Mountains in 1835." *American State Papers,* Military Affairs, Vol. 6, 24th Cong., 1st sess., No. 654 (1861).

"Massacre of the Cheyenne Indians." *Report of the Joint Committee on the Conduct of the War. Senate Report No. 142,* 38th Cong., 2d sess. (1865).

Proceedings of Council Held September 18, 1859, by Agent Thomas Twiss, Deer Creek, N.T. House Executive Document No. 61, 36th Cong., 1st sess. (1860).

Reports of the Commissioner of Indian Affairs, 1824–1889.

"The Sand Creek Massacre." *Report of the Secretary of War. Senate Executive Document No. 26,* 39th Cong., 2d sess. (1867).

Testimony Taken by a Select Committee of the Senate Concerning the Removal of the Northern Cheyenne Indians. Senate Report No. 78, 46th Cong., 2d sess. (1880).

"Treaties with Several Tribes." *American State Papers,* Indian Affairs, Vol. 2, 19th Cong., 1st sess., No. 226 (1826).

United States Statutes at Large, Vol. 15.

GOVERNMENT DOCUMENTS

UNPUBLISHED

Documents Relating to Negotiations of Indian Treaties, 1801–69 (microfilm, 10 reels).

Records of the War Department:
Office of the Adjutant General, Letters Received, 1855–59, 1868.
United States Army Commands, Department of the Missouri, Fort Hays, Letters Sent.
Report of Secretary of War, 1878.

Records of the Bureau of Indian Affairs:
Central Superintendency, Letters Received.
Central Superintendency, Letters Sent.
Cheyenne and Arapaho Indians.
Upper Arkansas Agency, Letters Received.
Upper Platte Agency, Letters Received.
Office of Indian Affairs, Letters Received.
Office of Indian Affairs, Letters Sent.

Catalogue Card in Photo File. Cheyenne Indians. Bureau of Ethnology

NEWSPAPERS

Cheyenne Transporter (Darlington Agency, I.T.)
Chicago Times
Chicago Tribune
Cincinnati Commercial
Cincinnati Gazette
Daily National Intelligencer (Washington, D.C.)
The Daily Times (Leavenworth)
Kansas Daily Tribune (Lawrence)
Kansas Weekly Tribune (Lawrence)
Missouri Democrat (Saint Louis)
Missouri Republican (Saint Louis)
New York Herald
New York Times
New York Tribune
Washington Evening Star (Washington, D.C.)
Washington National Republican (Washington, D.C.)
Wichita Eagle
Winfield Courier (Kansas)

Index

Abert, Lieut. James W.: sketch of Yellow Wolf, 28; leads exploring party, 31; sketches Indians at Bent's Fort, 31, 32; becomes acquainted with Yellow Wolf, 32; meets Slim Face, 35; at Bent's Fort, 50–51
Adobe Walls: 154; *see also* battle of Adobe Walls
Ahtunowhiho (One Who Lives Below): 6
Alights-on-the-Cloud (Cheyenne): at Fort Laramie council, 52; killed, 53, 55–56, 144; photograph, 54; in Washington, D.C., 55; chosen to go to Washington, D.C., 60; Indian names given, 168n.
Alvord, Capt. Henry, reports on Cheyennes: 118
Antelope Hills: 118–20
Anthony, Maj. Scott: commanding Fort Lyon, 65; "Red-Eye Chief," 110–11
Apache Indians: 55, 68, 107; *see also* Plains Apache Indians
Arapaho Indians: 5, 10, 19, 21, 30, 55–56, 86, 90, 94, 97–98, 101, 107, 109–10, 112, 115, 118–19, 150, 166n.; raids against Comanches and Kiowas, 29; invasion of lands, 61, 63; lodges, 68; new reservation, 113; attack Kiowas, 117; at Fetterman Massacre, 127; treaty, 127–28; soldier societies, 144; delegation to Washington,

D.C., 148; name for Little Wolf, 174n.
Archer, Ambrose (captive): 109
Arickara Indians: *see* Arikara Indians
Arickaree Fork of Republican River: 31
Arickaree River: 94, 98, 101
Arikara Indians: 20, 25
Arkansas River: 5, 15, 21, 25–28, 30–31, 33–34, 50–51, 56, 60–63, 65, 68–69, 85, 96, 112, 114, 117, 119, 123, 133, 145
Armor, worn by Alights-on-the-Cloud: 53
Around (Cheyenne): 48–49
Ash Hollow: 60
Assiniboine Indians: 20
Atkinson, Gen. Henry: 23–24, 104
Avo-na-co (Lean Bear): 170

Bannock Indians: 131
Baptist meeting: 96
Bark: *see* Bear's Feather and Old Bark
Barnum, P. T.: 74; invites Indian delegation to New York, 73; Great Mogul, 75; Museum, 75
Battle of Adobe Walls: 5, 154, 160
Battle of Beecher's Island: 5, 94, 101–102
Battle of Little Bighorn: 5
Battle of Platte Bridge: 166n.
Battle of Washita: 5, 94
Battle of Wolf Creek: 5, 49

Lone Wolf (Kiowa): makes trip to Washington, D.C., 69; visits White House, 70
Long expedition: 21

McCusker, Philip: photographs, 40, 142
McGillycuddy, V. T. (Sioux agent): 140
Mackenzie, Charles (trader): 5; meets Cheyennes, 18, 19
Mackenzie, Col. Ranald S.: 5, 134; attacks Northern Cheyennes, 131
Mad Wolf (Southern Cheyenne): photograph, 40
Magpie (Southern Cheyenne): photograph, 80
Man-to-toh-pa: see Four Bears
Mandan Indians: 16, 18–19; villages, 17; robe story, 165n.
Ma-nim-ic: see Minimic
Man-on-a-Cloud (Southern Cheyenne): photograph, 40
Man-That-Stands-on-the-Ground (Northern Cheyenne): 175n.
Marble, Daniel (captive): 109
Mead, J. R.: describes Black Kettle, 172n.
Medicine Arrow (Cheyenne): 13
Medicine Arrows: 12, 90, 93, 105, 115–16, 145, 158, 168n.
Medicine Lodge Creek: 12, 89, 93, 100, 115, 117, 128
Medicine Lodge council: 92, 101, 104, 145, 150, 158
Medicine Lodge, Kans.: 154
Medicine Water (Cheyenne): 53; war party leader, 148
Menimick (Southern Cheyenne): see Minimic
Me-tu-ra-to (Black Kettle): 173n.
Mexican traders: 20, 25, 53
Miles, John D. (Cheyenne and Arapaho agent): 132, 161; photograph, 40, 42; takes delegation to Washington D.C., 128; develops grass-lease plan, 148, 155; confiscates guns and ammunition, 154; resigns, 156
Miles, Gen. Nelson A.: 52, 58, 134, 138; visits Fort Reno, 156
Minimic (Southern Cheyenne): signs treaty, 113; quoted, 143; peace leader, 144; at Camp Supply, 146, 158, 160; at agency, 152; delivers letter to Fort Lyon, 157; at Medicine Lodge council, 158; photograph, 159; victim of circumstance, 160; sent to prison, 160; dies, 161; names, 177n.
Minnesota region: 15
Minniconjou Sioux: 138
Minnimic: see Minimic
Min-nin-ne-wah (Whirlwind): 169n.
Mississippi River: 163
Missouri Republican: 53; covers Fort Laramie treaty, 49
Missouri River: 15–16, 18, 20, 23, 128
Moka-ta-va-tah: see Black Kettle
Moke-tav-a-to: see Black Kettle
Moke-ta-ve-to: see Black Kettle
Moke-to-ve-to: see Black Kettle
Mo-ko-va-ot-o: see Black Kettle
Montana, state of: 137, 141
Mooers, Asst. Surgeon J. H.: wounded at Beecher's Island, 102
Morning Star (Northern Cheyenne): see Dull Knife
Mo-ta-vato: see Black Kettle
Moving Behind (Cheyenne woman): 174n.
Moving Whirlwind (Cheyenne): 169n.; see also Whirlwind
Mun-a-men-ick: see Minimic
Murphy, Thomas (Indian Superintendent): 100

between Lincoln and Indians, 70
Washita Massacre: 36, 143, 150; *see also* Battle of Washita
Washita River: 8–9, 94, 104–105, 119–20, 144–45, 156, 158
Watonga, Okla.: 80, 83
Wessells, Capt. Henry: 134–35
Whirlwind (Arapaho): finds gold, 56
Whirlwind (Cheyenne, the earlier): 169n.
Whirlwind (Cheyenne, the latter): photograph, 41, 44, 45, 46, 57; Southern Cheyenne chief, 58; at Darlington, 58; visits Washington, D.C., 128, 148; band of, 146; at agency, 148, 152
White Antelope (Southern Cheyenne): 5, 9, 53, 106, 109, 111–12, 168–169n.; photograph, 54, 64, 108; early years, 59; as Dog Soldier, 59; chief in 1842, 60; at Bent's Fort, 61; on upper Saline, 61; at Fort Wise, 61; refuses invitation, 63; makes speech, 63–65; goes to Fort Lyon, 65; killed at Sand Creek, 65
Whiskey: Porcupine Bear talk on, 47; Cheyenne enemies do not drink, 48; large amount sold at Fort Laramie, 48; disposed of, 50; peddlers, 117
White Bull (Cheyenne): 166n.
White Bull (Kiowa): trip to Washington, D.C., 69; visits White House, 70
White Clay Creek: 133
White Cow (Northern Cheyenne): 28, 168n.
White Crow (Northern Cheyenne): brings in captive, 124; signs treaty of 1868, 128, 168–69n.

White Eagle (newspaper): 161
White Elk (Northern Cheyenne): tells of massacre, 127
White father: 16; *see also* Great Chief, President of U.S.
White Horse (Cheyenne): 87, 114; photograph, 44, 147; at Beecher's Island, 94, 101–103; at Medicine Lodge council, 117; head of band, 146; goes to Washington, D.C., 141; at Camp Supply, 160
White House: 55, 70, 73
Whiteley, Simeon (Indian agent): 172n.
White Man's Chief (Cheyenne): 26
White Powder (Northern Cheyenne): 175n.
White River: 95
White Shield: photograph, 40, 151; head of band, 146; goes to Washington, D.C., 148; comes to agency permanently, 148; settles near Cantonment, 155; refuses grass-lease plan, 155
Wichita Indians: 115, 119
Wichita, Kans.: 113, 150, 161, 172n.
Wild Hog (Northern Cheyenne): 131, 136; photograph, xii
Wind spirits: 6
Wo-he-hiv: *see* Dull Knife
Wokai-hwo-ko-mas: *see* White Antelope
Wolf Chief (Cheyenne): 106
Wolf Creek (Oklahoma): 30, 59, 105, 115, 120, 146
Wolf Face (Cheyenne): photograph, 42
Wolf Fire (Northern Cheyenne): captured, 124
Wolf Left Hand (Northern Cheyenne): at Fetterman Massacre, 127

205